Study Skills for Fourth Grade
Table of Contents

Introduction 2
Letter to Parents 4
Strategies for Success 5
Assessment 6

Following Directions 9

Using Reference Materials
Pronunciation 11
Dictionary and Encyclopedia 14
Maps and Charts 18

Becoming Familiar with Story and Book Parts
Index and Glossary 23
Book Parts 26
Character 28
Plot 31
Setting 33

Understanding Literature
Forms of Literature 35
Figurative and Literal Language 37
Fact and Opinion 39
Cause and Effect 47
Predicting Outcomes 55

Strengthening Reading Comprehension
Main Idea 59
Facts 67
Sequence 75
Summary 83
Conclusion 87

Answer Key 95

Study Skills for Fourth Grade
Introduction

Study Skills for Fourth Grade is designed to provide practice with and reinforcement of the thinking skills and strategies necessary for success at this grade level. It also reinforces the skills necessary for standardized achievement tests.

This book concentrates on the fundamentals of learning at this level. From following directions to the parts of a book, these are basics that all students need to know before they can move on to higher levels of thinking in these areas. This book is designed to give students the practice necessary to build strong foundations in understanding. Once these skills are mastered, students will be more likely to achieve success as they move forward.

Organization

This book is organized into five main areas for study: Following Directions, Using Reference Materials, Becoming Familiar with Story and Book Parts, Understanding Literature, and Strengthening Reading Comprehension. Each section focuses on important areas for skills reinforcement. There is a letter for the teacher to send to the parents which explains the purpose of the worksheets in this book. You will find a handy strategies chart which will help students stay focused on their work and keep it in perspective. The assessment can be given as a pre-test or post-test to evaluate improvement.

Use

This book is designed for independent use by students. Copies of the activities can be given to individuals, pairs of students, or small groups for completion. They can also be used as a center activity.

To begin, determine the implementation that fits your students' needs and your classroom structure. The following plan suggests a format for implementation.

1. **Explain** the purpose of these activities to the class. You may want to discuss any questions students may have.

2. **Do** a practice activity together. Most sections have a page of explanation and practice that lends itself to guided practice. Go over the explanation with the students, let them try the practice activity, and then discuss the activity as a class.

3. **Assign** pages of the unit for independent or small group study or for homework. The sections are

designed so that no activity is more than two pages long. Many activities are one-page assignments.

4. Determine how you will monitor the assessment. Decide whether you want to administer the assessment as a pre-test and post-test to keep in the students' portfolios, or if you want only to administer the test when the students complete the book. You may also wish to use the test to determine which students need reinforcement in certain areas and which students may already have mastered these skills.

Additional Notes

1. Parent Communication Sign and send the Letter to Parents home with your students, and encourage your students to share the letter with their parents. This will alert parents that their children may be bringing home papers for homework. It will encourage parents to become involved with the homework and help the child form good study habits. If the work is completed at school, decide if it will go into the students' portfolios for discussion at conference time.

2. Student Communication Assure the students that these worksheets are for practice purposes to help them improve their study skills. Make copies of the *Strategies for Success* to pass out to the students, and post it on the wall for easy reference. As a class, talk about other strategies that could be included.

3. Make it Fun Make the work fun and meaningful when possible. For example, after a discussion and work with maps and charts, find a way to relate the information to the students' own lives. Think about your own town and how the students can use mapping skills to explain the way to their own house. Go on a field trip, take notes, and make a giant floor map of part of your town. If your class is doing a school project or there is a national event that has caught the interest of the class, take a survey and make a chart so that students can see their skills working in a real-life situation. Do a mixed-up play in which small groups get together independently and make up a plot, setting, and characters. When they get together, see how the pieces fit together. They may have placed cowboys on a spaceship in a plot to rid the world of pollution forever!

Dear Parent:

Strong basic skills are important for all students. With study and practice of the basic skills, students have a much higher chance for achieving success as they move ahead through school.

We will be using *Study Skills for Fourth Grade* to work on and strengthen those skills necessary for success in the fourth grade. We will discuss the skills in class, and then have pages for independent study. These pages may be completed in class, or they may be given as homework.

If your child brings work home, please consider the following suggestions:

- **Provide a quiet place to work.**
- **Go over the directions together.**
- **Encourage your child to do his or her best.**
- **Be available for questions should your child become confused or need some assistance. Remind your child to do just what the directions state.**
- **Check the lesson when it is complete. Note improvements as well as concerns.**

Help your child maintain a positive attitude about study skills. Let your child know that each lesson provides an opportunity to learn and grow. If your child expresses anxiety about these skills, help him or her understand what causes the stress. Talk about ways to deal with the anxiety.

Above all, enjoy this time you spend with your child. He or she will feel your support, and skills will improve with each activity completed.

Thank you for your help!

Cordially,

Strategies for Success

Purpose Set a realistic goal. Develop a plan.

Planning How much time do you have to achieve your goal?
Use your time well.

Prioritizing Review what you need to do.
Decide what needs to be done first, second, and so on.

Persistence Work toward your goal each day.
Don't give up.

Practice In sports, crafts, music, or schoolwork, training is very important.
Keep at it.

Pacing Study each day.
Don't wait until the last minute.

Name _____   Date _____

Study Skills for Fourth Grade
Assessment

 **DIRECTIONS:**

Read each question carefully. Follow the directions for each question.

1. Put a star next to your name at the top of this page. Draw a circle around the star. Draw a square around the page number.

2. Fill in the answer circle in front of the word that goes with the phonetic respelling.
   a. char' kol'   ⓐ chuckle   ⓑ channel   ⓒ champion   ⓓ charcoal
   b. sek' end   ⓐ scream   ⓑ sector   ⓒ second   ⓓ scold

3. Which word would be found on a dictionary page with the guide words *may* and *medicine*?   ⓐ maximum   ⓑ mutter   ⓒ measure   ⓓ myth

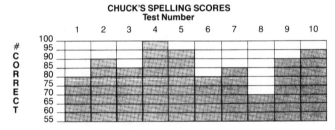

4. Use the chart to answer the questions.
   A. What was Chuck's best score? _____
   B. On what test did he get it? _____

5. Write *index*, *glossary*, *table of contents*, or *title page* next to where you think you would look for the following information.
   A. the name of the author of a book _____
   B. what information is discussed in Chapter 2 _____
   C. what the term "cubic" means _____
   D. how many pages mention "deserts" _____

6. Read the following passage and then answer the question. Write your answer on the line.

   Steve ran all the way home from school. He couldn't wait to see his mother and his new baby brother. He was sure they would be home from the hospital by now.

   How do you think Steve feels? _____

Name _____   Date _____

Assessment (p. 2)

7. Read the following story and then number the events in the order in which they really happened.

    Beth was in a hurry. Her mother was waiting at the front door of the store. As she was going to buy her last present, she saw a little girl crying. Beth remembered the day she had been lost in a department store. She had been with her mother. Suddenly, she hadn't been able to find her mother. She had started crying. She remembered how happy she had been when the clerk helped her find her mother. Beth went to the little girl and asked if she was lost. When the girl said yes, Beth looked for a clerk to help them. Beth was late to meet her mother, but when her mother found out what had happened, she was not upset.

    a. _____ Beth remembered being lost.
    b. _____ Beth started crying.
    c. _____ Beth met her mother by the front door.
    d. _____ Beth saw a little girl crying.
    e. _____ Beth was in a hurry to meet her mother.
    f. _____ Beth helped the little girl.

8. Read the story and decide *where* and *when* the story takes place. Write your answer on the line.

    Karla and her sister had just finished sliding down the tornado slide. They were on their way to the swings when Betty looked at her watch. It was almost time for them to go home for dinner.

    a. where _____
    b. when _____

9. Read the following sentences and decide if they are taken from *historical*, *realistic*, or *fantasy* stories. Write your answer on the line.
    a. Sandy caught five fish on the fishing trip. _____
    b. The magical broom sang and danced as it swept the floor. _____
    c. Laura and her family waited for the Pony Express to bring their mail. _____

10. Read the following sentences. Decide if each sentence is using *figurative* or *literal* language. Write your answer on the line.
    a. David ate a ton of food for lunch. _____
    b. The news was very upsetting to us. _____
    c. The woman's neck was as long as a giraffe's. _____
    d. Tina is hard to get along with when she gets mad. _____

Name _____   Date _____

Assessment (p. 3)

11. Read the following sentences. Decide if they are *fact* or *opinion*. Write your answer on the line.
    a. The world is round. _____
    b. I think my state is the best to live in. _____
    c. I fed a baby elephant at the zoo. _____
    d. The Art Museum was very boring. _____

12. Read the following sentences. Draw a line under the effect, and circle the cause.
    a. Bob didn't go because he had homework.
    b. As a result of the rain, the game was called off.

13. Read the following story. Predict what will happen next. Write your answer on the line in a complete sentence.

    Cindy liked the new town that she and her family had just moved to, but she still missed her best friend, Katie. She wanted to tell Katie everything that had happened since she had moved. Cindy's mother said it would cost too much money to call Katie. Cindy got out some paper, a pen, and an envelope.

    What will happen next? _____
    _____

14. Read this paragraph and find the main idea. Fill in the answer circle next to the main idea of this paragraph.

    Mike carefully placed the good dishes on the table. He put the silverware next to each plate, just as his mother had shown him. He set two candles in the middle of the table. He wanted everything to be perfect for his grandfather's birthday party.

    This story is mainly about
    ⓐ the present Mike bought his grandfather.
    ⓑ Mike setting the table for his grandfather's party.
    ⓒ the correct way to set a table for a party.
    ⓓ Mike putting candles in the middle of the table.

15. Write one sentence that is a summary of the following selection.

    Charles and his friends went fishing all afternoon. Mike caught two fish. Pat caught three. John caught five. Charles only caught one, but it was the biggest.

    _____

Name _____ Date _____

FIRST DO THIS, THEN DO THAT

Many times people make mistakes because they do not follow directions carefully. Written directions are often not followed because the following rules are ignored:

1. Directions should always be read carefully.

Very often people don't read the directions because they are sure they already know what to do. Read the directions anyway, just to be sure.

2. Read all of the directions before doing anything.

This will help you understand what you are going to do. It will also prevent you from getting too far along before you realize there is something else you might need to do.

3. Directions should always be followed in the order that they are given.

Doing things out of order can change the way things turn out.

> **To Follow Directions:**
> 1. READ all of the directions carefully *before* you start.
> 2. FOLLOW all directions in the order they are given.

DIRECTIONS:

Follow these directions exactly. Make your drawing on another sheet of paper.

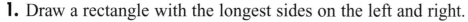

1. Draw a rectangle with the longest sides on the left and right.
2. Inside the rectangle draw two small squares next to each other near the top. Do not let the squares touch each other or the sides or top of the rectangle.
3. In each square, put a + sign that touches the top and sides of the square.
4. Put an upside-down V on top of the rectangle. Make the upside-down V touch the top corners of the rectangle.
5. Draw another small square inside the rectangle that touches the bottom. Draw a line down the middle of this square.
6. What have you drawn?

Following Directions

Name _____   Date _____

STEP BY STEP

DIRECTIONS:

Follow these directions exactly. Make your drawing at the bottom of this page.

1. Draw an oval about the size of an egg. Draw it lying on its side.
2. Print two capital W's under the oval, one near each end. Make the top of the W's touch the bottom of the oval.
3. Draw a medium-sized circle that touches the left side of the oval.
4. Put a smaller circle in the middle of the circle you just drew.
5. Draw two smaller circles inside the circle you just drew in step #4.
6. Draw two small triangles touching the top of the larger circle you drew in step #3.
7. Draw an S near the upper right-hand side of the first oval. Make the end touch the oval.
8. Add two small circles touching sides above the small circle you drew in step #4.
9. Draw a dot in each of the two small circles you just drew.
10. What animal have you drawn?

Following Directions

Name _____   Date _____

HOW DO YOU SAY THAT?

Say this word aloud.   **imply**

How do you know how to say or pronounce a word that is new to you? If you are not sure how to say a word, you can look in the dictionary to find out how it should be pronounced. The word you look up in the dictionary is called the entry word. It is written in a dark type. The entry word is divided into syllables by dots.

im • ply (im • plī´)

After the entry word, the phonetic respelling is given. The word is spelled in symbols that help you pronounce the word. These symbols are explained in a pronunciation key that appears on every other page of the dictionary.

By using the pronunciation key, you know that the first syllable of *imply* has the same vowel sound as the *i* in the word *it*. The second syllable has the same vowel sound as the *i* in the word *ice*. You also can tell that the second syllable is pronounced more strongly because of the accent mark (´) after that syllable in the phonetic respelling.

a	add	i	it	o͝o	took	oi	oil
ā	ace	ī	ice	o͞o	pool	ou	pout
â	care	o	odd	u	up	ng	ring
ä	palm	ō	open	û	burn	th	thin
e	end	ô	order	yo͞o	fuse	th	this
ē	equal					zh	vision

ə = { a in *above*   e in *sicken*   i in *possible*
      o in *melon*   u in *circus* }

HBJ School Dictionary

To Pronounce New Words:
1. **FIND** the entry word in the dictionary.
2. **LOOK** at the way it is divided into syllables.
3. **FIND** the phonetic respelling.
4. **USE** the pronunciation key.
5. **DECIDE** which syllable is spoken most strongly.
6. **SAY** the new word.

DIRECTIONS:

Draw a line around the word that goes with each phonetic respelling.

1. (bāt)   back   beat   bait
2. (skâr´ē) share   scary   scream

Name _____ Date _____

PROPER PRONUNCIATION

DIRECTIONS:

Look at the list of phonetic respellings on the left. Then read the words on the right. Match the phonetic respelling with the correct word on the right. Write the letter of the word in front of its phonetic respelling. Use the pronunciation key to help you.

_____ 1. tā´lər   a. usual
_____ 2. ri·sûrch´   b. thousand
_____ 3. thou´zənd   c. nervous
_____ 4. nach´ər·əl d. lucky
_____ 5. fō´nə·graf´ e. tailor
_____ 6. luk´ē   f. backstage
_____ 7. di·zīn´   g. create
_____ 8. ə·tach´   h. alarm
_____ 9. bak´stāj´   i. design
_____ 10. yōō´zhōō·əl j. cloth
_____ 11. trezh´ər   k. research
_____ 12. nur´vəs   l. attach
_____ 13. klôth   m. natural
_____ 14. ə·lärm´   n. limestone
_____ 15. līm´stōn´ o. treasure
_____ 16. krē·āt´   p. phonograph

a	add	i	it	o͝o	took	oi	oil
ā	ace	ī	ice	o͞o	pool	ou	pout
â	care	o	odd	u	up	ng	ring
ä	palm	ō	open	û	burn	th	thin
e	end	ô	order	yōō	fuse	ŧħ	this
ē	equal					zh	vision

ə = { a in *above*   e in *sicken*   i in *possible*
      o in *melon*   u in *circus*

HBJ School Dictionary

Name _____ Date _____

SOUNDING IT OUT

DIRECTIONS:

Fill in the answer circle in front of the word that goes with the phonetic respelling.

1. kə·lek´shən
   - ⓐ collection
   - ⓑ carnival
   - ⓒ kennel
   - ⓓ kerchief

2. bī´sik·əl
   - ⓐ beyond
   - ⓑ battery
   - ⓒ bicycle
   - ⓓ bushel

3. kûr´tən
   - ⓐ curtain
   - ⓑ kitten
   - ⓒ channel
   - ⓓ knobby

4. ô´ning
   - ⓐ awning
   - ⓑ onward
   - ⓒ oblong
   - ⓓ orchard

5. chär´kol´
   - ⓐ chuckle
   - ⓑ channel
   - ⓒ champion
   - ⓓ charcoal

6. ē´zəl
   - ⓐ easy
   - ⓑ easel
   - ⓒ equal
   - ⓓ exhaust

7. ber´ē
   - ⓐ beady
   - ⓑ bury
   - ⓒ beyond
   - ⓓ breathe

8. ak·tiv´ə·tē
   - ⓐ awkward
   - ⓑ acorn
   - ⓒ actress
   - ⓓ activity

9. vol´yəm
   - ⓐ vehicle
   - ⓑ volume
   - ⓒ victim
   - ⓓ velvet

10. sek´ənd
    - ⓐ scream
    - ⓑ sector
    - ⓒ second
    - ⓓ scold

Pronunciation

Name_____   Date_____

LOOKING IT UP

A dictionary is a book in which words are listed in alphabetical order, along with each word's pronunciation, part of speech, and meaning. Look at this entry from a dictionary for the word *mischief.*

    mis • chief [mis´chif] n.   1. Harmful teasing.   2. Trouble.

The word *mischief* is printed in dark type. Next the pronunciation is given. The *n.* after the pronunciation tells you what part of speech the word is. *Mischief* is a noun. Finally, the entry gives two definitions, or meanings, for the word *mischief.* Many words have two or more meanings.

DIRECTIONS:

Look up these words in a dictionary. Write each word's meaning. If the word has more than one meaning, only write the *first* meaning given.

1. camouflage _____

2. demonstrate _____

3. disguise _____

4. lattice _____

5. ornery _____

6. quality _____

7. substance _____

Name _____   Date _____

FINDING MEANINGS

DIRECTIONS:

Look up these words in a dictionary. *First,* write the meaning of the word. If the word has more than one meaning, only write the first one given. *Second,* write a sentence using the word as it is defined in the meaning you wrote.

1. baffle _____
   _____

2. blunder _____
   _____

3. crude _____
   _____

4. dignity _____
   _____

5. exterior _____
   _____

6. lounge _____
   _____

Dictionary and Encyclopedia

GUIDE WORDS

A dictionary is an important source of information. It can tell you how to spell a word, how to pronounce a word, what part of speech a word is, and the meaning or meanings of a word. The words are listed in alphabetical order. Each dictionary page has two words at the top of the page. These two words are called guide words. They can help you find words faster. The first guide word tells you the first word that is listed on that page. When you are looking for a word, you should look at the guide words. Decide if the word you are looking for comes in between those two words in alphabetical order.

Look at these two guide words.   **heave   human**

What if you were looking for the word *help*? Would it be listed on this page? Yes, the word *help* comes between the words *heave* and *human* when they are put in alphabetical order. What about the word *handsome*? No, that word would be on a page before this one. It comes before the word *heave* when they are put in alphabetical order. How about *hurt*? No, it would come after the word *human*. It would be on a page after this one.

> **To Use Guide Words in a Dictionary:**
> 1. **THINK** about what letters the word you are looking for starts with.
> 2. **LOOK** at the guide words to see if the word would come between the two words if they were listed in alphabetical order.

DIRECTIONS:

Look at these guide words. Then circle the words that you would find listed on that page.

      may   **medicine**

meet	mechanics	matter	maximum
mat	million	mean	measure
meal	milk	mayor	myth
mutter	maze	mad	meant

Name_____   Date_____

VOLUMES OF INFORMATION

An encyclopedia is like a dictionary in several ways. Its subjects are listed in alphabetical order. Each subject is in dark print, followed by information about the subject. Often guide words are used on each page just as they are in a dictionary.

The biggest difference between a dictionary and an encyclopedia is the amount of information you will find. For example, if you looked up the word *cat* in a dictionary, you would find only a few lines giving the definition of a cat. If you looked up *cat* in an encyclopedia, you might find pages and pages about different kinds of cats. Another major difference is that an encyclopedia only discusses *topics*. It does not define common words as a dictionary does. As you know, an encyclopedia is usually made up of several volumes of books. When you are looking for information, you must know which volume to use. The outside of an encyclopedia tells you what beginning letters are included in each volume. They act much like guide words do in a dictionary. You must decide if what you are looking for comes between those letters if they were listed in alphabetical order. Look how this set of encyclopedia would look when it is in order on a shelf.

Vol. 1 A-C	Vol. 2 D-G	Vol. 3 H-L	Vol. 4 M-O	Vol. 5 P-R	Vol. 6 S-U	Vol. 7 V-Z

DIRECTIONS:

Write which volume number you would look in for information on the following:

_____ 1. France
_____ 2. trees
_____ 3. whales
_____ 4. birds
_____ 5. music

_____ 6. United Nations
_____ 7. kangaroos
_____ 8. Newfoundland
_____ 9. zebras
_____ 10. insect

Dictionary and Encyclopedia

Name _____ Date _____

READING A GRAPH

Often graphic sources such as maps, diagrams, and graphs are skipped over by readers because they look hard to understand. They are not hard to understand if you take a few minutes to look at them carefully. Graphs can give you more information in less space than the written word. But they must be studied before you can understand the information shown in them. Here are some steps you should follow when using graphic sources.

> **To Use Graphic Sources:**
> 1. **READ** the title carefully. What is it all about?
> 2. **READ** all of the labels. Take time to figure out what they mean.
> 3. **DECIDE** what it means. What does the graphic source tell you? What do you know now that you didn't before?

Study the bar graph and answer the questions that follow.

Chuck made a bar graph showing his scores on the spelling tests he had taken that year.

CHUCK'S SPELLING SCORES

1. What was Chuck's lowest score?   a. _____
   On what test did he get it?   b. _____

2. What was Chuck's best score?   a. _____
   On what test did he get it?   b. _____

3. On which two tests did Chuck   a. _____
   get 80% correct?   b. _____

4. What was Chuck's score on test 5? a. _____
   What was Chuck's score on test 10? b. _____

Name _____ Date _____

READING A MAP

DIRECTIONS: Study the map of Dogville. Then answer the questions.

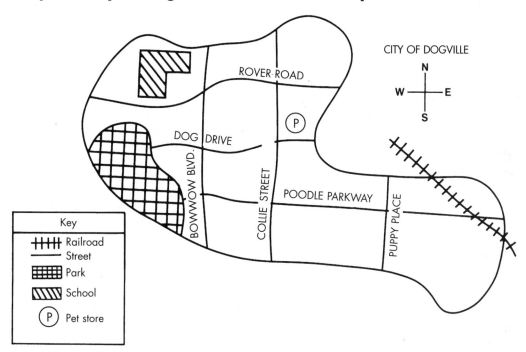

Which three streets go north and south?

_____ _____ _____
        (1)   (2)   (3)

Which three streets go east and west?

_____ _____ _____
        (4)   (5)   (6)

Which street crosses the railroad? _____
                                        (7)

The school is at the corner of _____ and _____
                                      (8)   (9)

Which street goes to the pet store? _____
                                          (10)

Name _____ Date _____

READING A TABLE

 **DIRECTIONS:**

Read the steps below.

> **To Use Graphic Sources:**
> 1. READ the title carefully.
> 2. READ all the labels.
> 3. DECIDE what they mean.

Read each question. Using the table, choose the correct answer to each question. Fill in the answer circle in front of your answer.

NUMBER OF SIT-UPS

		Monday	Tuesday	Wednesday	Thursday	Friday
C H I L D R E N	Nancy	18	21	23	28	30
	Tim	32	40	41	45	47
	Larry	21	27	32	34	35
	Beth	28	32	35	32	33

1. How many sit-ups did Beth do on Tuesday?
  ⓐ 28   ⓑ 35   ⓒ 21   ⓓ 32

2. Who did the most sit-ups on Friday?
  ⓐ Nancy   ⓑ Tim   ⓒ Larry   ⓓ Beth

3. On what day did Larry do the most sit-ups?
  ⓐ Monday   ⓑ Tuesday   ⓒ Thursday   ⓓ Friday

4. How many sit-ups did Nancy do altogether?
  ⓐ 205   ⓑ 120   ⓒ 90   ⓓ 99

Name _____   Date _____

LET'S TAKE THE BUS!

 **DIRECTIONS:**

Read each question. Using the table, choose the correct answer to each question. Fill in the answer circle in front of your answers.

BUS SCHEDULE			
Dallas to Houston		**Houston to Dallas**	
Leave	Arrive	Leave	Arrive
7:00 A.M.	12:30 P.M.	8:00 A.M.	1:30 P.M.
12:00 noon	5:30 P.M.	11:00 A.M.	4:30 P.M.
4:00 P.M.	9:30 P.M.	3:30 P.M.	8:00 P.M.

1. What time does the bus that leaves Dallas at 7:00 A.M. arrive in Houston?
   - ⓐ 12:30 P.M.
   - ⓑ 1:30 P.M.
   - ⓒ 5:30 P.M.
   - ⓓ 4:30 P.M.

2. What time does the last bus from Houston to Dallas leave Houston?
   - ⓐ 12:00 noon
   - ⓑ 4:00 P.M.
   - ⓒ 11:00 A.M.
   - ⓓ 3:30 P.M.

3. What time does the first bus leave from Dallas to Houston?
   - ⓐ 8:00 A.M.
   - ⓑ 7:00 A.M.
   - ⓒ 12:00 noon
   - ⓓ 11:00 A.M.

4. What time does the last bus arrive in Dallas?
   - ⓐ 4:30 P.M.
   - ⓑ 1:30 P.M.
   - ⓒ 3:30 P.M.
   - ⓓ 8:00 P.M.

Name _____ Date _____

FINDING YOUR WAY

 **DIRECTIONS:**

Study the map below. Choose the correct answer to each question. Fill in the answer circle in front of your answer.

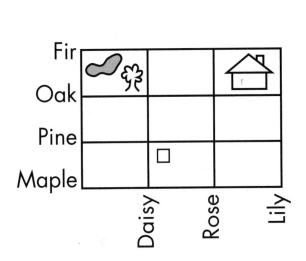

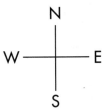

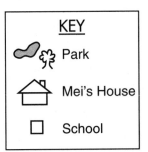

1. The school is on the corner of _____.
   - ⓐ Fir and Daisy
   - ⓑ Oak and Rose
   - ⓒ Pine and Lily
   - ⓓ Daisy and Pine

2. Which of the following streets runs north and south?
   - ⓐ Oak
   - ⓑ Maple
   - ⓒ Rose
   - ⓓ Fir

3. The park is on which street?
   - ⓐ Lily
   - ⓑ Rose
   - ⓒ Oak
   - ⓓ Maple

Name_____   Date_____

BOOK ENDS

There are several different parts of a book. Most of your textbooks probably have an index and a glossary. These are important parts of a book.

The index is almost always at the end of a book. It lists topics, names, etc., that are discussed in the book. These are listed in alphabetical order. Next to each topic or name is the page number, or numbers, where each topic or name is discussed. An index is helpful to you when you need to find specific information in a book, or want to know if the book has any information on a certain topic.

The glossary is a small dictionary also placed at the end of a book. It is just like a dictionary, except that it only lists and defines words that are hard or unusual in that particular book. The glossary is useful when you want to know the exact definition of a word, or when you want to know how a word is pronounced.

To Use the Index and Glossary:
1. **THINK** about the information you need.
2. **DECIDE** if the information you need can be found in the index or the glossary.
3. **LOOK** for the information.

DIRECTIONS:

Write *index* or *glossary* next to where you would look for the following information.

1. how to pronounce "Malaysia" _____

2. on what page "brown bears" are discussed _____

3. if the book discusses "pyramids" _____

4. what the term "cubic" means _____

5. if the book has information on "quartz" rocks _____

6. how to pronounce "plasma" _____

7. how many pages mention "deserts" _____

8. what the word "dense" means _____

Name _____   Date _____

USING AN INDEX

 **DIRECTIONS:**

Read the following page from an index of a book about trees. Then answer the questions that follow.

INDEX

Ashes:
  Black, 142
  Blue, 144
  Green, 145
  Mountain, 146
  Red, 143
  White, 141
Hickories:
  Bitternut, 131
  Mockernut, 130
  Pecan, 129
  Scarlet Haw, 132
  Shagbark, 133

Pines:
  Eastern White, 19
  Jack, 26
  Jersey, 23
  Lodgepole, 20
  Longleaf, 22
  Pinyon, 25
  Pitch, 21
  Ponderosa, 24
  Sugar, 17
  Virginia, 18
  Western White, 16
  Western Yellow, 15

List the page number where you would find information on the following trees:

_____ 1. Green Ash
_____ 2. Western Yellow Pine
_____ 3. Pecan Hickory
_____ 4. Lodgepole Pine
_____ 5. Red Ash
_____ 6. Ponderosa Pine
_____ 7. White Ash
_____ 8. Shagbark Hickory
_____ 9. Jersey Pine
_____ 10. Virginia Pine

Index and Glossary
Study Skills 4, SV 8052-9

© Steck-Vaughn Company

Name _____ Date _____

USING A GLOSSARY

 **DIRECTIONS:**

Look at this section of a glossary from a book about trees. Then answer the questions that follow.

GLOSSARY

arbor [är′bər] n. A place shaded by trees.
arboretum [är′bə·rē′təm] n. A plot of land on which trees are studied and/or displayed.
botany [bot′ə·nē] n. The science which collects, studies, and explains facts about plants and plant life.
cambium [kam′bē·əm] n. The soft tissue in such trees as the maple, elm, and ash, from which new wood and bark develop.
chlorophyll [klôr′ə·fil] n. The green coloring matter in plants.
coniferous [kō·nif′ər·əs] adj. Any cone-bearing tree, such as pine.
deciduous [di·sij′ oo·əs] adj. Any tree that sheds its leaves each year.
pith [pith] n. The loose spongy tissue inside the stem of a tree.

---

1. What word means *the soft tissue from which new wood can develop?* _____

2. What word means *a place shaded by trees?* _____

3. What word means *trees that shed their leaves?* _____

4. What word means *the tissue inside the stem of a tree?* _____

5. What word means *trees that have cones?* _____

6. What word means *the science that studies plant life?* _____

Name _____ Date _____

FINDING INFORMATION

DIRECTIONS:
Read the steps below.

To Use the Parts of a Book:
1. **THINK** about the information you need.
2. **DECIDE** where the information you need can be found.
3. **LOOK** for the information.

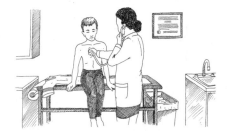

Read each incomplete sentence. Choose the part of a book that would be most helpful in finding the information. Fill in the answer circle in front of your answer.

1. To find the meaning of the word *unconscious* in your health book, you would look in the _____.
   ⓐ glossary   ⓑ table of contents   ⓒ index   ⓓ title page

2. To find the name of the author of a book, you would look in the _____.
   ⓐ glossary   ⓑ table of contents   ⓒ index   ⓓ title page

3. To find what information is discussed in Chapter Two of a book, you would look in the _____.
   ⓐ glossary   ⓑ table of contents   ⓒ index   ⓓ title page

4. To see if your health book has information on the common cold, you would look in the _____.
   ⓐ glossary   ⓑ table of contents   ⓒ index   ⓓ title page

5. To see what company published the book you are reading, you would look in the _____.
   ⓐ glossary   ⓑ table of contents   ⓒ index   ⓓ title page

Go on to next page.

FINDING INFORMATION (P. 2)

6. To see what page has information on blue whales in your science book, you would look in the _____.
    ⓐ glossary   ⓑ table of contents   ⓒ index   ⓓ title page

7. To see what year a book was published, you would look in the _____.
    ⓐ glossary   ⓑ table of contents   ⓒ index   ⓓ title page

8. If you were reading your science book and wanted to know how to pronounce the word *nitrogen,* you would look in the _____.
    ⓐ glossary   ⓑ table of contents   ⓒ index   ⓓ title page

9. To find what page Chapter 11 starts on, you would look in the _____.
    ⓐ glossary   ⓑ table of contents   ⓒ index   ⓓ title page

10. To see what part of speech the word *geography* is, you would look in the _____.
    ⓐ glossary   ⓑ table of contents   ⓒ index   ⓓ title page

Book Parts

Name _____ Date _____

WHO IS IN THE STORY?

Character

Characters in a story are simply the people or animals in the story. The main character in a story is whom the story is mostly about. The author of a story usually gives each character a certain personality. The qualities that make up the character's personality are called character traits.

DIRECTIONS:

Read the story and then answer the questions.

The tape player Charles wanted costs a lot of money. Charles had been saving his money for months so that he could buy it. Many times he was tempted to buy something else with his money, but his strong will had finally paid off. After saving and working for months, Charles finally had the money to get his tape player.

1. How would you describe Charles? _____

2. What is one of Charles' character traits? _____

> **To Understand the Feelings of Characters:**
> 1. READ the story carefully.
> 2. LOOK for clues to how the character feels.
> 3. THINK about how you would feel if it were happening to you.
> 4. DECIDE how the character feels.

Read each story below and write how you think the character feels on the line.

Betty tore the ribbon off the box. She couldn't believe her eyes as she opened the box. She had really gotten a kitten for her birthday.

3. How do you think Betty feels? _____

Nick hid his head in his pillows. He didn't think he would ever see his dog Hal again. Hal had been missing for over a week. Nick had looked everywhere.

4. How do you think Nick feels? _____

Name _____   Date _____

ABOUT CHARACTER

Read each story and then answer the questions.

    Nick had been worried about this test. He knew it was going to be hard. As he looked over at the teacher, he noticed that he was able to see Karen's paper. Karen was the smartest kid in the class. The teacher was busy grading other papers and wouldn't see if Nick took one peek. But when he thought for a minute, he knew that would be the wrong thing to do. Besides, Nick wanted to see how well he could do on this test by himself. Later, Nick was pleased with himself. He had gotten a B on the test without cheating. He might have gotten an A if he had cheated, but he wouldn't have felt as proud of himself as he was with the B that he had earned.

1. Who is the main character of this story? _____

2. Who are the other characters in the story? _____
_____

3. How would you describe Nick? _____
_____

4. Why did Nick decide not to cheat? _____
_____

5. How did Nick feel when he got a B on his test? _____
_____

6. What do you think is the theme of this story? _____
_____

HOW DO THEY FEEL?

DIRECTIONS:

Read each story below and write how you think the character feels on the line.

Kathy covered her eyes with her hands. She leaned over to her father and said, "I can't watch." She didn't want to see what the terrible monster in the movie would do next.

1. How do you think Kathy feels? _____

Bob didn't know what had come over him. He had never said such mean things to anyone, and to have said them to his best friend Mark! Bob picked up the phone to call Mark. He hoped that Mark would forgive him.

2. How do you think Bob feels? _____

Cindy couldn't believe it when her teacher said her name. She had really won the Tall Tales Writing Contest. She smiled as she went to the front of the room to get her ribbon.

3. How do you think Cindy feels? _____

David shouted to Paul, "You always get your way! You never do anything I want to do!"

4. How do you think David feels? _____

Steve ran all the way home from school. He couldn't wait to see his mother and his new baby brother. He was sure they would be home from the hospital by now.

5. How do you think Steve feels? _____

Nancy had been saving her last piece of candy for after supper. She knew her brother had eaten all of his. When she went to get her candy, it was gone! She ran to her brother's room.

6. How do you think Nancy feels? _____

Name _____   Date _____

GETTING IT STRAIGHT

You know how important it is to understand the sequence, or order of events, in a story or in directions you are trying to follow. Sometimes an author jumps around in time when telling a story. For example, suppose a boy in a story is reminded of something that happened a long time ago. The author may jump back in time and explain what had happened in the past. The boy in the story would be having a flashback, or remembering something that happened in the past.

> **To Understand Flashbacks in a Story:**
> 1. **READ** the story carefully.
> 2. **THINK** about what is happening in the story.
> 3. **DECIDE** if it is happening now or if it is a flashback.

DIRECTIONS:

Read the following story. Think about the sequence of events.

Tim was on his way to a baseball game when he saw a hungry and frightened little kitten hiding in some bushes. The little kitten reminded him of the day when he had found Max. Tim had only been five. He had been playing with his older brother in a field near their house. He had heard a small meow coming from a ditch. He had gone over and picked up the kitten. It was hungry and frightened. He had taken the kitten home and asked his mother if he could keep him. She hadn't really wanted to, but before long he was a part of the family. They had named him Max. Max and Tim became best friends. Max had been hit by a car about a year ago. He had died soon after. Tim went over to where the little kitten was. He picked him up and took him home.

Put the events in order as they really happened to Tim. Some are already ordered for you:

a. _____   Max became part of the family.
b. _____   Tim was on his way to a baseball game.
c. _____   Tim picked up the kitten and took him home.
d. __1__   Tim was five years old.
e. _____   He saw a kitten in the ditch.
f. __5__   Max got hit by a car and died.
g. _____   He saw a kitten in some bushes.
h. _____   The kitten reminded him of the day he found Max.
i. _____   He took it home and called it Max.

© Steck-Vaughn Company

31

Plot

Study Skills 4, SV 8052-9

Name _____   Date _____

ALL IN ORDER

DIRECTIONS:

Read the following story. Put the events in order as they really happened to Beth. Some of the events are already ordered for you.

Beth was in a hurry. She had to meet her mother by the front door of the department store in ten minutes. She still wanted to look at a few more things before she decided what she would buy her father for his birthday.

Just as Beth was going toward the sporting goods department, she noticed a little girl crying. Beth could see that there wasn't anyone nearby. Beth wondered if the little girl was lost. Beth remembered the day she had been lost in a store. She had been about six years old. She had been looking at furniture with her mother. Beth had sat down on a chair for a minute. When she had looked for her mother, she couldn't find her. She had started crying. Beth remembered how happy she was when a clerk had come over and helped her find her mother. Beth went over to the little girl and asked her if she was lost. When the little girl said yes, Beth looked for a clerk to help them.

Beth was a few minutes late meeting her mother by the front door, but her mother wasn't upset with her when she heard what had happened. She took Beth back into the store so Beth could find a present for her father.

a. _____ Beth remembered being lost.
b. _____ Beth started crying.
c. _____ Beth met her mother by the front door.
d. _____ A clerk helped Beth find her mother.
e. __1__ Beth and her mother were looking at furniture.
f. _____ Beth saw a little girl crying.
g. _____ Beth was on her way to the sporting goods section.
h. _____ Beth was in a hurry to meet her mother.
i. _____ Beth sat on a chair.
j. _____ Beth couldn't find her mother.
k. _____ Beth helped the little girl.
l. __12__ Beth and her mother bought a present.

Plot

Name _____   Date _____

WHERE AND WHEN?

DIRECTIONS:

Read the following story. Think about *where* and *when* the story takes place.

It was a hot, summer day. After Marty helped his mother clean the dishes from lunch, they decided to go swimming. Marty went to his bedroom to get his bathing suit.

Where does this story take place? If you said "at Marty's house" then you are right. You did a good job of picturing Marty and his mother cleaning up the kitchen and getting ready to go swimming.

When does this story take place? If you said "on a summer afternoon," you are right. You knew that Marty and his mother had just eaten lunch, and the story tells you that it was summer. Sometimes an author will tell you in more detail when a story takes place, such as the year, or the time of day.

> **To Determine Where and When a Story Takes Place:**
> 1. **READ** the story carefully.
> 2. **LOOK** for clues that tell you where and when the story takes place.
> 3. **DECIDE** where and when the story takes place.

Now read each story and decide *where* and *when* the story takes place.

After an early breakfast, Mike and his family started to pack. They put the tent and stove away in the truck. Then they went down to the lake for one last swim before they headed for home.

1. where _____
2. when _____

The first bell rang as Cindy took off her heavy coat and boots. She brushed the snow off her pants and got her books. She knew she had time to get a drink of water before class started.

3. where _____
4. when _____

Name _____   Date _____

STORY SETTINGS

DIRECTIONS:

Read the following stories and decide *where* and *when* they take place.

Barry was very excited. This was the first time his parents had let him stay up until 12:00 at night. He and his family sat in the living room and watched as the clock struck 12:00, bringing in a new year.

1. where _____
2. when _____

Patty took a shower and put on her pajamas. She went downstairs to say goodnight to her grandparents. She missed her parents already but knew she was going to enjoy visiting her grandparents and helping them around the farm.

3. where _____
4. when _____

Karla and her sister had just finished sliding down the tornado slide. They were on their way to the swings when Betty looked at her watch. It was almost time for them to go home for dinner.

5. where _____
6. when _____

Zorf looked at his calendar as he landed his spaceship on the planet Xmpet. He was able to determine that the year on Xmpet was 8437.

7. where _____
8. when _____

Janet and her father were enjoying their drive. The leaves on the trees were beginning to turn red, orange, and yellow. The sun was shining, but there was a coolness in the air. They decided they would stop and eat lunch at the next restaurant they saw.

9. where _____
10. when _____

WHAT KIND OF STORY IS IT?

You know that nonfiction is based on facts. You also know that fiction is literature that is made up. But did you know that there are three major types of fiction? Let's look closely at what they are.

Historical Fiction is a story about real people or real events, but with made-up details. There are two kinds of historical fiction. One has real characters from the past who are involved in made-up events and have conversations that are made up. The other involves real events, but has made-up characters.

Realistic Fiction is a story that is made up, but it could have really happened. There is nothing in the story that couldn't really happen.

Fantasy is a story that is clearly not true. It includes things that are impossible in real life. Fairy tales, myths, legends, and science fiction are all fantasy stories.

DIRECTIONS:

Read the following sentences, and write if they are taken from *historical*, *realistic*, or *fantasy* stories.

1. The fairy appeared in Kate's room without any warning. _____

2. Tom later became a drummer boy in the Civil War. _____

3. Tim and Jack went looking for the lost puppy. _____

4. The movie was the best the girls had seen. _____

5. The beautiful unicorn pranced in the clearing. _____

6. Maggie stood in a line of women waiting to vote for the first time in history. _____

Forms of Literature

FACT OR FICTION?

DIRECTIONS:

Read the following sentences, and write if they are taken from *historical, realistic,* or *fantasy* stories.

1. George Washington asked his mother if he could chop down a cherry tree.
   _____

2. Mark and his family were getting ready to go camping when the storm came.
   _____

3. Sandy caught five fish on the fishing trip.
   _____

4. The monster ate eighteen trees for lunch.
   _____

5. The wizard waved his hand and disappeared instantly.
   _____

6. As young Abe Lincoln read his book that night, he wondered what it would be like to travel across the country.
   _____

7. The magical broom sang and danced as it swept the floor.
   _____

8. The boys trembled when they heard the loud crash.
   _____

9. Laura and her family waited for the Pony Express to bring their mail.
   _____

10. The little sparrow flew as fast as he could to warn Harry of the danger ahead.
    _____

Name _____   Date _____

HE ATE HOW MUCH?

DIRECTIONS:

Read these two sentences. Think about what they mean.

1. The baby's smile was as wide as the ocean.
2. The baby had a big smile on its face.

How are these two sentences alike? Yes, they are both talking about a baby's big smile. How are they different? The first one uses figurative language. Could the baby's smile be as wide as the ocean? Of course not. The author has exaggerated how big the baby's smile was in order to make the sentence more interesting.

The second sentence is an example of literal language. The sentence means just what it says. The first one doesn't literally mean what it says.

To Tell the Difference Between Figurative and Literal Language:
1. **READ** the sentence carefully.
2. **THINK** about the meaning of the sentence.
3. **DECIDE** if the sentence says just what it means (literal), or if the sentence has exaggerated what it means (figurative).

Read the following sentences. Decide if they are using *figurative* or *literal* language. Write your answer on the line.

_____ 1. David ate a ton of food for lunch.

_____ 2. David ate a big lunch.

_____ 3. The woman had a long neck.

_____ 4. The woman's neck was as long as a giraffe's.

_____ 5. The news hit us like a bomb.

_____ 6. The news was very upsetting to us.

_____ 7. Tina is a monster when she gets mad.

_____ 8. Tina is hard to get along with when she gets mad.

_____ 9. The building was so tall it touched the sky.

_____ 10. The building was very tall.

Figurative and Literal Language

Name _____   Date _____

WHAT YOU REALLY MEAN IS

DIRECTIONS:

Each of the following sentences is an example of figurative language. Write a literal sentence below each sentence to tell what the sentence really means.

1. John had been in the pool for weeks.
   _____

2. Mother carries everything but the kitchen sink in her purse.
   _____

3. When Tom speaks, you can hear him a mile away.
   _____

4. Elsie turns into a fish when she gets into the water.
   _____

5. Carl's brain must have been on the moon when he said that.
   _____

6. As the plane went higher, the people on the ground turned into ants.
   _____

7. The man was as skinny as a rail.
   _____

8. It takes an army to wake Bob up.
   _____

9. Karen was beginning to melt from the heat.
   _____

10. I jumped out of my skin when Doug scared me.
    _____

Figurative and Literal Language

Name _____ Date _____

IS THAT A FACT?

DIRECTIONS:

Read the following three passages. Think about how they are different.

1. Abraham Lincoln was the 16th president of the United States. He lived from 1809-1865.
2. The largest penguin is the emperor penguin. It can be as large as three and one half feet tall.
3. The boy's eyes grew large as he stepped onto the spaceship. The "people" inside had two heads with sixteen eyes on each.

How are the three passages different? If you said that the first and second passages are nonfiction, and the third is fiction, you are right. Nonfiction writing is based on facts. Fiction is something that has been made up.

The first passage could be from a special kind of nonfiction book called a biography. Biographies are one of the most popular kinds of nonfiction books. A biography is a true story about someone's life. Many famous people have had at least one biography written about them.

The second passage could be from an informational book about penguins. Your science, social studies, and history books are also examples of nonfiction. So are encyclopedias. A nonfiction book is any book that gives you *facts*.

To Decide If What You are Reading is Fiction or Nonfiction:
1. READ the story carefully.
2. THINK about its meaning.
3. DECIDE if what you are reading is fiction (made up) or nonfiction (based on facts).

Read each statement and decide if it is fiction or nonfiction. Write *fiction* or *nonfiction* before each statement.

1. _____ George Washington was the first president of the United States.

2. _____ The state of Washington produces more apples than any other state in the nation.

3. _____ Mark got on the magic carpet and took a ride.

Fact and Opinion

Name_____   Date_____

DID YOU MAKE THAT UP?

DIRECTIONS:

Read each statement and decide if it is fiction or nonfiction. Write *fiction* or *nonfiction* before each statement.

1. _____ All of the animals of the forest decided to have a meeting.

2. _____ The Bureau of Engraving and Printing produces all the paper money used in the United States.

3. _____ Dr. James Naismith invented basketball in 1891.

4. _____ Golden eagles watch the ground for rabbits and other small animals.

5. _____ Gail used her magic powers to make herself invisible.

6. _____ In 1940, only 10,000 TV sets existed. Today there are tens of millions of sets.

7. _____ A kangaroo is a large leaping animal that lives in Australia.

8. _____ The giant was as tall as a three-story building.

9. _____ The monster was green with purple eyes.

10. _____ The year was 2089, and people were living in spaceships.

11. _____ Memorial Day is a day set aside to honor the soldiers and sailors who have died since the Civil War.

12. _____ The mermaid helped the girl swim to the top of the water.

13. _____ William Shakespeare was an author who lived from 1564-1616. Many of the things he wrote are still read today.

14. _____ February 14th is St. Valentine's Day, a day when many people send greetings to their family and friends.

Go on to the next page.

Fact or Opinion

Name _____   Date _____

DID YOU MAKE THAT UP? (P. 2)

15. _____ People who cannot hear can communicate by using their hands. This method of communication is called sign language.

16. _____ Frostbite is caused by being out in the cold for too long without proper clothing.

17. _____ The mouse ran to the street so he could watch the parade.

18. _____ The fairy promised the little girl that three of her wishes would come true.

19. _____ A fire fighter is a person whose job is putting out fires.

20. _____ Oranges, apples, peaches, and pears are only a few of the kinds of fruits grown in the United States.

21. _____ Thomas Jefferson was the third president of the United States. He lived from 1743-1826.

22. _____ A gorilla is the largest member of the ape family. Most gorillas live in western Africa.

23. _____ The birds were busy helping Cynthia make a dress to wear to the ball.

24. _____ Henry Ford was the person who started the Ford Motor Company. He lived from 1863-1947.

25. _____ The whale carried the little boy across the ocean.

26. _____ In 1930, Ruth Wakefield, a woman who worked in an inn in Massachusetts, invented the chocolate chip cookie.

27. _____ Dolphins, whales, and manatees are mammals that live in water, but breathe air.

28. _____ The giant bird offered to take Michael for a ride.

Fact or Opinion

Name _____ Date _____

YOUR TURN

DIRECTIONS:

Make up a short story about you and some of your friends. Make sure the story is make-believe, or fiction.

1. _____
_____
_____
_____
_____
_____
_____
_____

Write a short autobiography. Include where and when you were born, some information about your family, and what you like to do in your spare time. Make sure everything you write is *true*, not make-believe.

2. _____
_____
_____
_____
_____
_____
_____

Name _____ Date _____

THAT'S WHAT YOU THINK

 **Read the steps below.**

> To Distinguish Between Facts and Opinions:
> 1. READ the sentence carefully.
> 2. THINK about its meaning.
> 3. LOOK for clue words (think, believe, feel, etc.).
> 4. DECIDE whether it is a fact or an opinion.

Read each selection to yourself. Choose the correct answer to each question. Fill in the answer circle in front of your answer.

    Raccoons are cute and fun to watch. They have a funny face that looks like they have a mask over it. Raccoons are very playful. They are often seen around campgrounds. They come out at night looking for handouts from campers. If they don't find handouts, they may steal food from the campsite, so be careful! Raccoons normally eat frogs, shrimp, and other shellfish. I think their favorite food is corn. They often raid corn fields. When raccoons become frightened, they make a very strange sound. It is something like a long whistle, but it is so high-pitched that humans can hardly hear it. Tamed raccoons make excellent house pets. Although they are a playful and gentle animal, wild raccoons can be very tough fighters when they are cornered, so you should always be careful.

1. Which of the following is a statement of <u>opinion</u>?
   ⓐ Raccoons are often seen around campgrounds.
   ⓑ Raccoons eat frogs, shrimp, and other shellfish.
   ⓒ Raccoons make a strange sound when they are frightened.
   ⓓ Raccoons are cute and fun to watch.

2. Which of the following is a statement of <u>fact</u>?
   ⓐ I think their favorite food is corn.
   ⓑ Tamed raccoons make excellent house pets.
   ⓒ Raccoons never raid corn fields.
   ⓓ Raccoons are cute and fun to watch.

Go on to the next page.

THAT'S WHAT YOU THINK (P. 2)

I had a great time on our vacation to Indianapolis. We went there to visit my Uncle Charlie. The first day we were there, Uncle Charlie took us to the Indianapolis Motor Speedway and Museum. That is where the Indianapolis 500 car race is held every Memorial Day weekend. The cars we saw were the neatest in the world. The next day we went to the Children's Museum. There was a mummy, toy trains, and a whole merry-go-round right in the museum! The Children's Museum was the greatest! Two days later we went to the Indianapolis Museum of Art. Mom and Dad liked it, but I thought that museum was very boring. Things got better the next day when we went to the Indianapolis Zoo. We rode on a train that took us all around the zoo. I even got to feed a baby elephant. I think Indianapolis is a great place to visit.

3. Which of the following is a statement of <u>fact</u>?
   ⓐ I think Indianapolis is a great place to visit.
   ⓑ The cars we saw were the neatest in the world.
   ⓒ We went there to visit my Uncle Charlie.
   ⓓ I thought the museum was very boring.

4. Which of the following is a statement of <u>opinion</u>?
   ⓐ We went to the Children's Museum.
   ⓑ The Indianapolis 500 is held every Memorial Day weekend.
   ⓒ We rode a train at the Indianapolis Zoo.
   ⓓ I think Indianapolis is a great place to visit.

5. Which of the following is a statement of <u>fact</u>?
   ⓐ I fed a baby elephant at the zoo.
   ⓑ The Art Museum was very boring.
   ⓒ I think Indianapolis is a great place to visit.
   ⓓ The Children's Museum was the greatest.

Fact and Opinion

IN MY OPINION

Read each selection to yourself. Choose the correct answer to each question. Fill in the answer circle in front of your answer.

Japan is an interesting country. Its capital city, Tokyo, is the world's second largest city. Japan is one of the world's biggest fishing countries. The country supplies one sixth of the fish caught in the world! The clothes that the Japanese wear on special occasions are very pretty. They are called kimonos. A kimono is a one-piece, loose-fitting garment with wide sleeves. It is folded over in front and held together by a sash that is called an obi. Japanese food is delicious. Rice and fish are the basic foods in Japan. Learning about Japan and its customs is fun.

1. Which of the following is a statement of opinion?
   ⓐ Learning about Japan and its customs is fun.
   ⓑ Tokyo is the world's second largest city.
   ⓒ Rice and fish are the basic foods in Japan.
   ⓓ Japan supplies one sixth of the fish caught in the world.

2. Which of the following is a statement of fact?
   ⓐ Japan is an interesting country.
   ⓑ Tokyo is the capital city of Japan.
   ⓒ Japanese clothes are very pretty.
   ⓓ Learning about Japan and its customs is fun.

3. Which of the following is a statement of opinion?
   ⓐ Rice and fish are the basic foods in Japan.
   ⓑ Japanese food is delicious.
   ⓒ A sash is called an obi.
   ⓓ A kimono is worn on special occasions.

Go on to the next page.

Name _____   Date _____

IN MY OPINION (P. 2)

   I think basketball is the most exciting game to watch or play. Dr. James Naismith invented basketball in 1891. The first baskets were two fruit baskets hung at each end of a gym in Springfield, Massachusetts. Many things have changed in the game of basketball since then. Some of the rules have been changed. Today, the basket is a metal hoop with a net made of cord. The object of the game is still the same, to put the ball through the basket more times than the other team.

   Everyone should try playing basketball. It is fun to dribble a ball down the court. There is no better feeling than making a basket.

4. Which of the following is a statement of opinion?
   ⓐ Some of the rules have changed in basketball.
   ⓑ Dr. James Naismith invented basketball.
   ⓒ Everyone should try playing basketball.
   ⓓ The first baskets were fruit baskets.

5. Which of the following is a statement of fact?
   ⓐ Today, the basket is a metal hoop with a net made of cord.
   ⓑ Basketball is the most exciting game to watch or play.
   ⓒ There is no better feeling than making a basket.
   ⓓ Everyone should try playing basketball.

6. Which of the following is a statement of opinion?
   ⓐ It is fun to dribble a ball down the court.
   ⓑ The object of the game is still the same.
   ⓒ Today, the basket is a metal hoop with a net made of cord.
   ⓓ Some of the rules have been changed.

Fact and Opinion

Name _____ Date _____

WHAT AND WHY

 **DIRECTIONS:**

Read this sentence and think about what happened.

The rabbit ran away because it was frightened.

Which part of the sentence tells you what happened? Yes, <u>the rabbit ran away</u> tells you what happened. Which part of the sentence tells you why it happened? Yes, <u>because it was frightened</u> tells you why the rabbit ran away. The part of the sentence that tells you why something happened is the cause. The part of the sentence that tells you what happened is called the effect. The <u>cause</u> always happens <u>first</u>. The <u>effect</u> always happens <u>after</u> the cause. Look at the sentence again.

The rabbit ran away / because it was frightened.
      effect   cause

Which word in the sentence gives a clue as to which part of the sentence is the cause? Yes, the word <u>because</u> is a clue word. Here are some clue words that will help you find the cause and the effect.

CLUE WORDS

cause	effect
1. because	1. therefore
2. since	2. thus
	3. so

To Understand Cause and Effect:
1. READ the sentence carefully.
2. LOOK for clue words.
3. DECIDE which part is the cause and which is the effect.

Sometimes there is one effect and several causes. Read the sentences. Underline the effect, and draw a line around the two causes.

1. Bob didn't go because he had homework, and he was tired.

2. As a result of the cold and rain, the game was called off.

3. Tim was saving his money since he wanted to buy a new ball and a new bat.

Go on to the next page.

Cause and Effect

Name _____   Date _____

WHAT AND WHY (P. 2)

DIRECTIONS:

Read each story and the questions that follow. Underline the effect, and then write your answers on the lines. Use complete sentences.

David was very hungry. He hadn't eaten much breakfast. He had been playing hard all morning. He made a large sandwich and fixed a big bowl of fruit.

What are two reasons (causes) for the effect?

4. _____

_____

5. _____

_____

Martha did very well on the history test. She had read the chapter twice. Then her mother had asked her questions about what was in the chapter.

What are two reasons (causes) for the effect?

6. _____

_____

7. _____

_____

Robert had cleaned the garage. He had raked the leaves. His parents gave him $7.00 for his work. He needed money for a new toy he wanted.

What are two reasons (causes) for the effect?

8. _____

_____

9. _____

_____

Cause and Effect

Name _____ Date _____

FINDING OUT WHY

 **DIRECTIONS:**

Read each story and the questions that follow. Underline the effect, and then write your answer on the lines. Use complete sentences.

Eddie asked his parents if they could go camping on the weekend. The weather was supposed to be very nice. The park where they usually camped was having a special nature program for boys and girls his age. Eddie also wanted to go because he had a new fishing pole he hadn't used yet. He couldn't wait to try out his new pole at the lake. Eddie was very happy when his parents agreed to go camping.

What are three reasons (causes) for the effect?

1. _____
   _____

2. _____
   _____

3. _____
   _____

Pauline was late for school. There had been a power failure during the night, so the alarm hadn't gone off. Then Pauline's baby brother had cut his finger and had to be taken care of. Finally, Pauline and her mother got in the car to go to school, but the car wouldn't start. Pauline hoped that the day would get better.

What are three reasons (causes) for the effect?

4. _____
   _____

5. _____
   _____

6. _____
   _____

Go on to the next page.

Cause and Effect

Name _____ Date _____

FINDING OUT WHY (P. 2)

DIRECTIONS:

Read each story and the questions that follow. Underline the effect, and then write your answer on the lines. Use complete sentences.

Linda had carefully planted the seeds in the spring. She had watered the garden when it didn't rain enough. She had spent many hours weeding the garden. Linda's flower garden was beautiful.

What are three reasons (causes) for the effect?

7. _____

8. _____

9. _____

Janice's favorite subject is math. She has always enjoyed helping her younger brother do his math assignments. She also likes to help her math teacher check the math tests after school. Janice is going to study to be a math teacher.

What are three reasons (causes) for the effect?

10. _____

11. _____

12. _____

Cause and Effect

Name _____ Date _____

LOOKING FOR THE CAUSE

Read the steps below.

> To Identify Cause and Effect:
> 1. READ the passage carefully.
> 2. LOOK for clue words such as <u>because</u> and <u>since</u>.
> 3. DECIDE which part is the cause (what happened) and which is the effect (why it happened).

Read each selection. Choose the correct answer to complete each sentence. Fill in the answer circle in front of your answer.

    Tom put on his scout uniform. He checked himself in the mirror. He wanted to look good tonight since he was going to be given an award by his scout troop. Tom won the award because he had saved a young boy from drowning. The young boy had been in a rowboat that turned over because he leaned over too far. Tom knew the boy was in trouble because he wasn't wearing a life jacket and was yelling for help. Since Tom had learned lifesaving in scouting, he knew what to do. He had rowed his boat near the boy and turned the boat toward the boy, stern first. Then he had the boy grab the stern and hold on while Tom rowed him to shore.

1. Tom was getting an award because he had _____.
   - ⓐ won more badges than anyone else
   - ⓑ saved a boy from drowning
   - ⓒ won a swimming contest
   - ⓓ won a boat race

2. Since Tom was getting an award tonight, he _____.
   - ⓐ wanted to look his best
   - ⓑ was very nervous
   - ⓒ bought a new suit
   - ⓓ prepared a speech

3. The rowboat turned over because _____.
   - ⓐ the young boy leaned over too far
   - ⓑ he had rowed his boat near the boy
   - ⓒ he had the boy grab the stern
   - ⓓ he wasn't wearing a life jacket

Go on to the next page.

Name _____ Date _____

LOOKING FOR THE CAUSE (p. 2)

DIRECTIONS:

Read each selection. Choose the correct answer to complete each sentence. Fill in the answer circle in front of your answer.

Kathy's first day at summer camp had not gone very well. She was supposed to be put in the same cabin as her friend Nancy. She wasn't put in the same cabin as Nancy because the counselor had made a mistake. Since the counselor had promised that they could be together, she had Kathy trade places with someone in Nancy's cabin. Because of the time it took Kathy to move, she missed the morning swim. After all that trouble, Nancy had to go home because she got the measles. As Kathy got ready for bed, she realized she had forgotten her pillow. The counselor gave her one, but Kathy had a hard time sleeping because the pillow was so lumpy. She hoped that things would start getting better tomorrow.

4. Because the counselor had made a mistake _____.
   ⓐ there wasn't enough food for everyone
   ⓑ Kathy and Nancy had to go home
   ⓒ Kathy and Nancy weren't put in the same cabin
   ⓓ the campers didn't get to go on a hike

5. Kathy missed the morning swim because _____.
   ⓐ of the time it took her to move
   ⓑ she forgot to bring her swimsuit
   ⓒ she wasn't feeling well
   ⓓ she didn't get up in time

6. Kathy had a hard time sleeping because _____.
   ⓐ she was homesick
   ⓑ the pillow was so lumpy
   ⓒ there was too much noise
   ⓓ she was afraid of the dark

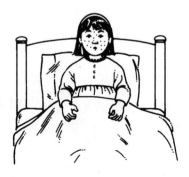

Cause and Effect

THAT'S BECAUSE

DIRECTIONS:

Read each selection. Choose the correct answer to complete each sentence. Fill in the answer circle in front of your answer.

In the 1700s, Daniel Bernoulli discovered something about air streams that has become known as Bernoulli's Principle. Since Daniel had grown up in a family of scientists, it wasn't surprising that he made such an important discovery. Daniel Bernoulli discovered that the slower the speed of a flowing liquid or gas, the higher the pressure. This was an important discovery since it explains how a plane can fly. A plane flies because an airplane wing is shaped so that the air flowing over the wing is faster than the air going under the wing. This makes the pressure below the wing higher than the pressure above the wing, and the higher pressure creates an upward force.

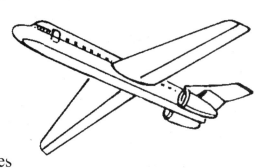

1. It wasn't surprising that Daniel made such an important discovery because _____.
   - ⓐ his father invented the airplane
   - ⓑ he lived near a stream
   - ⓒ his family were scientists
   - ⓓ he often built model airplanes

2. Daniel Bernoulli's discovery was important because it explains _____.
   - ⓐ why solids can float
   - ⓑ what causes windstorms
   - ⓒ the effects of atmospheric pressure
   - ⓓ why airplanes can fly

3. There is higher pressure under the wing because the _____.
   - ⓐ air travels more slowly
   - ⓑ wing weighs less than the plane
   - ⓒ wing is slightly curved
   - ⓓ gravity isn't as strong there

Go on to the next page.

Name _____ Date _____

THAT'S BECAUSE (P. 2)

DIRECTIONS:

Read each selection. Choose the correct answer to complete each sentence. Fill in the answer circle in front of your answer.

A geyser is a hot spring that often sends up jets of water and steam into the air. A geyser named Old Faithful is one of the most famous geysers. It is in the black sand basin of Yellowstone National Park. It shoots water and steam 100 to 150 feet into the air about every 70 to 90 minutes. Geologists believe that geysers are formed when melted rock meets underground water. The red-hot melted rocks cause the water to turn into steam. Because steam causes pressure, the steam and boiling water blow into the air. In some geysers the water is very hot. Because the water is so hot, it dissolves several minerals from the rocks it passes over. Since many people believe the minerals are good for them, some of these places have become health resorts.

4. Steam and boiling water blow into the air because _____.
- ⓐ the ground has eroded away
- ⓑ steam causes pressure
- ⓒ water weighs less than air
- ⓓ minerals make the water dissolve

5. Some places with mineral springs have become health resorts because _____.
- ⓐ the water makes unusual plants grow nearby
- ⓑ many people believe the minerals are good for them
- ⓒ a wide variety of wild animals is drawn to the spring
- ⓓ geysers are fun to watch

6. Several minerals from the rocks the water passes over are dissolved because _____.
- ⓐ people believe the minerals are good for them
- ⓑ steam causes pressure
- ⓒ some places have become health resorts
- ⓓ the water is so hot

Cause and Effect

Name _____   Date _____

WHAT WILL HAPPEN NEXT?

 **DIRECTIONS:**

Read the following story and think about what will happen next.

Gail was very dirty. She had spent the afternoon playing softball. It had been very hot. Gail went upstairs. She got a towel and washcloth. She turned the shower on.

What do you think will happen next? If you said that Gail would take a shower, you were right. You did a good job of using the information in the story and your own experiences to predict or decide what would probably happen next.

> **To Predict What Will Happen Next:**
> 1. **READ** the story carefully.
> 2. **THINK** about what is happening in the story.
> 3. Use the information in the story and your own past experiences to **DECIDE** what will probably happen next.

Read the following stories and predict what will happen next. Write your answers on the lines in a complete sentence.

As Nicole got everything ready to start building her model airplane, she realized she was almost out of glue. Nicole's mother was getting ready to go downtown. Nicole ran downstairs to catch her mother before she left.

1. What will happen next? _____

_____

It had been a very unusual winter. It hadn't snowed once. Ted had gotten a new sled for his birthday. He couldn't wait to try it out. One Saturday morning, Ted's brother woke him up. He told him to look outside. There was about six inches of snow on the ground. Ted hurried and got dressed. He ate his breakfast quickly. Then he put on his warm coat, hat, and mittens.

2. What will happen next? _____

_____

_____

_____

Predicting Outcomes

Name _____   Date _____

AND THEN WHAT?

 **Read each story and predict what will happen next. Write your answers in complete sentences.**

One of the things Roger did every night was put everything he needed for school the next day into his bag. Roger was just about to fall asleep when he realized he hadn't put his report into his bag. The report was due tomorrow. He was afraid he might forget it in the morning. Roger crawled out of bed.

1. What will happen next? _____
_____

Regina had asked her parents if she could have a kitten for her birthday. She had wanted one for several years, but her parents always said she had to wait until she was old enough to take care of one. She thought she was old enough now. When her birthday came, her parents said they were going to take her over to see her grandfather. On the way her father parked the car in front of the pet shop.

2. What will happen next? _____
_____

Cindy liked the new town that she and her family had just moved to, but she still missed her best friend, Katie. She wanted to tell Katie everything that had happened since she had moved. Cindy's mother said it would cost too much money to call Katie. Cindy got out some paper, a pen, and an envelope.

3. What will happen next? _____
_____

Predicting Outcomes

Name_____   Date_____

WHAT DO YOU THINK WILL HAPPEN?

DIRECTIONS:

Read each story and predict what will happen next. Write your answers in complete sentences.

The yard was covered with leaves. The leaves had all fallen off the tree yesterday during the storm. Doug and Justin got the rakes out of the garage.

1. What will happen next? _____
_____

Tom's friend had just called and invited him over for the afternoon. Tom remembered that his mother had told him he couldn't go anywhere until his room was cleaned. Tom ran upstairs to his room.

2. What will happen next? _____
_____

Adam's parents both got home late from work. There wasn't much food in the house. Adam's father said there was a new restaurant in town that he would like to try. Adam and his parents got in the car.

3. What will happen next? _____
_____

Diane helped her mother take down the pictures and move all the furniture to the middle of the room. Then they took the curtains down. They spread papers along the walls. Mother opened the can of paint with a screwdriver.

4. What will happen next? _____
_____

Go on to the next page.

Predicting Outcomes

Name _____   Date _____

WHAT DO YOU THINK WILL HAPPEN? (P. 2)

Read each story and predict what will happen next. Write your answers in complete sentences.

Bart had fallen off his bicycle. Sharon knew he may have broken his leg. She saw a telephone booth nearby. She was glad she had a quarter in her pocket.

5. What will happen next? _____

_____

Carl was getting ready to go fishing. He remembered that he had left his pole at David's house. He hoped David was home. He went to the telephone.

6. What will happen next? _____

_____

There was a movie that Elsie wanted to go to tomorrow afternoon. She had already spent this week's allowance. Sometimes her mother would give her extra money for doing odd jobs around the house. She had noticed that her mother's car needed washing. She went into the living room, where her mother was reading a book.

7. What will happen next? _____

_____

All Nancy could think about was going to sleep. She had felt sleepy all day. She had gone to the basketball game anyway. She had almost fallen asleep during the game! Afterward, her father asked her if she wanted to go get something to eat, but Nancy said no.

8. What will happen next? _____

_____

Predicting Outcomes

Name _____   Date _____

THE MAIN IDEA

 **DIRECTIONS:**

Read the following paragraph and think about its main idea.

Nancy's favorite game is chess. She also likes to play checkers and backgammon. She likes to play card games, too. Sometimes she plays "Fish" with her friend Carla.

How do you decide what the main idea of a paragraph is? First, you have to decide what the topic of the paragraph is. Then you have to decide what all of the other sentences are saying about the topic.

What is the topic of the paragraph you just read? Sure, Nancy playing games is the topic of the paragraph. What is it that all of the sentences in the paragraph are telling you about the topic? Each of the sentences tells you what kind of games Nancy likes to play. What is the main idea of the paragraph? It is that Nancy likes to play many kinds of games.

The main idea of the paragraph is not always stated directly in the paragraph. Sometimes the paragraph will only imply, or suggest, the main idea. When this happens, you must think of the main idea by reading the paragraph very carefully and thinking about what all of the sentences are saying about the topic.

> **To Find the Main Idea:**
> 1. **READ** the paragraph carefully.
> 2. **FIND** the topic of the paragraph.
> 3. **DECIDE** what all the sentences are saying about the topic.

Now read this paragraph and find the main idea. Remember, the main idea is not always stated directly in the paragraph.

Mark looked in the basement. He looked in the garage. He looked in his brother's room. Mark finally remembered that he had left his watch at his friend's house.

Fill in the answer circle next to the main idea of this paragraph.

ⓐ Mark looked in the basement and the garage.
ⓑ Mark looked at his friend's house.
ⓒ Mark's watch was at his brother's house.
ⓓ Mark couldn't find his watch.

Name _____   Date _____

MAKE A LONG STORY SHORT

DIRECTIONS:

Read each paragraph. Then answer the questions.

Ron was having a good time. He liked to watch the animals eat. He was glad he had come to the zoo in time to watch the animals get fed. They were much more active during feeding time.

1. What is the main idea of this paragraph?

_____

_____

Diane woke up early. She had several things to do today. She had to clean her room. Then she was going to a birthday party. Later she had a piano lesson. That evening she was going out to eat and to a movie with her parents.

2. What is the main idea of this paragraph?

_____

_____

Don likes to feel the water splash on his face. He enjoys sitting on the deck and feeling the sun warm his body. His favorite part is when his father lets him steer the sailboat.

3. What is the main idea of this paragraph?

_____

_____

Whenever someone needed to know how to spell a word, they always asked Juanita. Some of her friends called her a "walking dictionary." She had won the annual spelling bee at school for the past three years.

4. What is the main idea of this paragraph?

_____

_____

Name_____ Date_____

MORE MAIN IDEA

DIRECTIONS:

Read each story. Then answer the questions.

Teachers teach us how to become better readers. They teach us how to write. They also teach us how to do math. We can also learn about interesting people and places from teachers.

1. What is the main idea of this paragraph?

_____
_____

Paula's dog can sit up. It can also play dead. When she tells it to, the dog will stay where it is until Paula says the dog can move. The dog also can jump through a hoop.

2. What is the main idea of this paragraph?

_____
_____

Terri likes to read mysteries. She also enjoys books that make her laugh. Her favorite books are about horses. When Terri goes to the library she has a hard time choosing which book she will read that week.

3. What is the main idea of this paragraph?

_____
_____

Wesley likes to rock his baby sister to sleep. He also enjoys feeding his sister. His mother even taught him how to change the baby's diaper. Wesley's favorite thing to do is to play with his sister while his mother is busy doing other things.

4. What is the main idea of this paragraph?

_____
_____

Go on to the next page.

© Steck-Vaughn Company   61   Main Idea
                                        Study Skills 4, SV 8052-9

Name _____ Date _____

MORE MAIN IDEA (P. 2)

 **DIRECTIONS:**

Read each story. Fill in the answer circle in front of the correct answer to each question.

Dogs must be taken to a veterinarian for check-ups and shots. They also must be fed properly every day. Dogs need to be given an occasional bath. The owner of a dog must also make sure the dog gets enough exercise.

5. What is the main idea of this paragraph?
- ⓐ Dogs are expensive pets.
- ⓑ Dogs need to be taken on walks every day.
- ⓒ Dogs need a lot of care and attention.
- ⓓ Dogs are the best kind of pets.

Sharon needed to get some toothpaste at the drugstore. Then she had to stop by the shoe repair shop and pick up her mother's shoes. Next, she was going to buy some seeds at the garden shop.

6. What is the main idea of this paragraph?
- ⓐ Sharon needed to go to the garden shop.
- ⓑ Sharon had several errands to do.
- ⓒ Sharon was out of toothpaste.
- ⓓ Sharon's shoes needed to be repaired.

People, animals, and plants all need clean water to drink. Water also helps us keep ourselves, and everything else, clean. The best thing about water is how it feels when you jump into it on a hot summer day!

7. What is the main idea of this paragraph?
- ⓐ Our bodies need a lot of water.
- ⓑ Everything would be dirty if we didn't have water.
- ⓒ Swimming is fun on a hot summer day.
- ⓓ Water is useful in many different ways.

Name _____ Date _____

WHAT'S THE STORY?

 **Read the steps below.**

> **To Find the Main Idea:**
> 1. **READ** the paragraph carefully.
> 2. **FIND** the topic of the paragraph.
> 3. **DECIDE** what all the sentences are saying about the topic.

Read each story to yourself. Choose the correct answer to complete each sentence. Fill in the answer circle in front of your answer.

Mike carefully placed the good dishes on the table. He put the silverware next to each plate, just as his mother had shown him. He set two candles in the middle of the table. He wanted everything to be perfect for his grandfather's birthday party.

1. This story is mainly about _____.
   ⓐ the present Mike bought his grandfather
   ⓑ Mike setting the table for his grandfather's party
   ⓒ the correct way to set a table for a party
   ⓓ Mike putting candles in the middle of the table

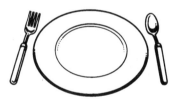

Sara took her dog to school. But this school wasn't for children; it was for dogs. With the help of special trainers, Sara was able to teach her dog to sit, come, lie down, and stay.

2. This story is mainly about _____.
   ⓐ Sara's dog winning a prize at school
   ⓑ Sara taking her dog to a special school
   ⓒ how dogs can help blind people get around
   ⓓ a school that has special children

Go on to the next page.

Main Idea

Name _____   Date _____

WHAT'S THE STORY? (P. 2)

DIRECTIONS:

Read each story to yourself. Choose the correct answer to complete each sentence. Fill in the answer circle in front of your answer.

Taking care of a small child is a big responsibility. Babysitters should know many things about the child, such as his or her likes and dislikes, before the parents leave. Babysitters should also know how to reach the parents, police, and fire department in case they are needed.

3. This story is mainly about _____.
  ⓐ children's likes and dislikes
  ⓑ how much babysitters can expect to be paid
  ⓒ things that babysitters should know
  ⓓ how to call the police and fire department

Rosita and her mother went to the grocery store. Then they went to pick up some clothes from the cleaners. After that, they went by the drug store to get some medicine for Rosita's sister. When they got home, Rosita was very tired.

4. This story is mainly about _____.
  ⓐ how sick Rosita's sister had been
  ⓑ the things Rosita and her mother forgot at the store
  ⓒ taking some clothes to the cleaners
  ⓓ the busy day that Rosita and her mother had

Chicago, Illinois, has lots of interesting museums. There are also two different zoos to visit. Many people enjoy swimming or boating in Lake Michigan. On a clear day, you can see for miles from the top of the Sears Tower. It is one of the world's tallest buildings.

5. This story is mainly about _____.
  ⓐ the world's tallest building
  ⓑ things that you can see in museums
  ⓒ the many things to do in Chicago
  ⓓ how many people live in Chicago

Main Idea

Name _____ Date _____

WHAT THE STORY IS SAYING

 **DIRECTIONS:**

Read each story to yourself. Choose the correct answer to complete each sentence. Fill in the answer circle in front of your answer.

Carol looked under the bed. She looked on her desk and everywhere else in her room. Then she went downstairs. She looked under the couch and behind the chairs. She could not remember where she had put her bag of marbles.

1. This story is mainly about _____.
   ⓐ Carol looking all over her room
   ⓑ Carol finding her marbles in the basement
   ⓒ Carol looking for her bag of marbles
   ⓓ Carol cleaning out her desk drawers

The fastest wind ever recorded was on Mount Washington in New Hampshire. In 1934, the wind blew 231 miles an hour across the top of the mountain. The wind is so fierce there that chains are anchored in solid rock to keep the weather station from blowing away.

2. This story is mainly about _____.
   ⓐ the highest mountain in the northeastern United States
   ⓑ a weather station on the top of Mount Washington
   ⓒ the fierce winds on the top of Mount Washington
   ⓓ a weather station that once blew away

Before the 1970s, people were allowed to kill as many alligators as they wanted. Many people sold the skins of the alligators to people who make shoes, belts, and handbags. Alligators almost disappeared. The alligators came back very quickly. Today there are laws that limit how many alligators can be killed in Louisiana and Florida.

3. This story is mainly about _____.
   ⓐ laws that exist in Louisiana and Florida
   ⓑ alligators and the laws that protect them
   ⓒ how to make shoes, belts, and handbags
   ⓓ how dangerous alligators can be

Go on to the next page.

Name _____   Date _____

WHAT THE STORY IS SAYING (P. 2)

DIRECTIONS:

Read each story to yourself. Choose the correct answer to complete each sentence. Fill in the answer circle in front of your answer.

Michael's favorite sport is basketball. He practices shooting baskets every day. He also likes soccer. He is on a soccer team at school. He is also a good runner. He hopes to be on the track team when he gets in high school.

4. This story is mainly about _____.
   ⓐ the kinds of sports that Michael enjoys
   ⓑ the rules of playing soccer
   ⓒ how much Michael likes to run
   ⓓ the soccer team at Michael's school

Jessica was a little nervous as she entered her new school. She knew that it would take a while to get used to everything. Jessica's mother took her to the principal's office to sign in. Then the principal took her to her new room. Her teacher was very nice. At recess, several children asked her to play with them.

5. This story is mainly about _____.
   ⓐ going to the principal's office
   ⓑ Jessica's first day at a new school
   ⓒ how much Jessica misses her old friends
   ⓓ the games Jessica likes to play at recess

It's in the Details

 **DIRECTIONS:**

Read the following selection.

The howler monkeys of South America are very interesting animals. They hardly ever leave the treetops. When they need a drink, they lick damp leaves. The howler monkeys got their name from the noise they make when they are scared. When they sense danger, they make a loud noise that can be heard up to three miles away. Their noise can often scare away what is threatening them.

What is the topic of the above selection? Yes, the topic is howler monkeys. What is the main idea? Yes, the main idea is that howler monkeys are interesting animals. Why are these monkeys interesting? The details of the above paragraph tell us why they are interesting. See if you can answer these questions about the details of the above paragraph. Look back at the paragraph if you need help.

1. How did the howler monkeys get their name?

_____

2. How do the howler monkeys get water to drink?

_____

Details are words and sentences that describe something. They can tell us "who," "what," "where," or "when." A detail supports the main idea.

Details add information to a story and make it more interesting. Often you are asked to remember details from a story.

> **To Recall Specific Facts and Details:**
> 1. READ the story carefully.
> 2. READ the question carefully.
> 3. THINK about what the question is asking.
> 4. REREAD the story if necessary to answer the question.

Write two sentences that give details about what you did last weekend.

3. _____

_____

Name _____ Date _____

READING CAREFULLY

DIRECTIONS:

Read the following selection and the questions that follow. Write the answers to the questions on the lines.

Tornadoes, sometimes called twisters or cyclones, have the fastest winds on record. A tornado can whirl winds as fast as 250 miles an hour. They can tear trees up by the roots and flatten whole towns. Tornadoes most often sweep across the central plains of the United States. They almost always come in the spring. That is because during the spring, warm air from the south crashes into cooler air from the north. When that happens, thunderstorms form, and sometimes the storms cause tornadoes.

1. What are two other names for tornadoes?
   _____

2. Where do tornadoes usually occur?
   _____

3. When do tornadoes usually occur?
   _____

4. How fast can winds go during a tornado?
   _____

5. What causes tornadoes?
   _____

6. What kind of damage can tornadoes do?
   _____

Facts

Name _____ Date _____

WHAT ARE THE FACTS?

DIRECTIONS:

Read the following selection and the questions that follow. Write the answers to the questions on the lines.

Every day we take many things for granted. One thing we take for granted is water. No plant or animal could live without water. It is needed for drinking, cleaning, and keeping us cool. Our bodies are about two thirds water. We need about a quart of water a day to replace the water we lose naturally. All the food we eat and the things we use every day required much water in their making.

Americans use a half trillion gallons of water a day. Each person in the United States uses about 90 gallons of water a day for cleaning and gardening. Two more gallons per person are used for drinking and cooking. Factories use lots of water to make goods. It takes 60,000 gallons of water to make one ton of steel. Farmers use 115 gallons of water to grow the wheat for one loaf of bread, and 4,000 gallons are needed to get one pound of beef. As you can see, water is very important to us all. We must always be sure to take care of the water we have.

1. What three things do humans use water for?
_____

2. How much of our bodies is water?
_____

3. How much water do people need to drink in one day?
_____

4. How many gallons of water do Americans use in one day?
_____

5. How many gallons does it take to make one loaf of bread?
_____

6. How many gallons does it take to get one pound of beef?
_____

Go on to the next page.

Name _____ Date _____

WHAT ARE THE FACTS? (P. 2)

DIRECTIONS:

Read the following selection and the questions that follow. Write the answers to the questions on the lines.

Hawks, falcons, and eagles are raptors. That means they are birds that look for small animals on the ground to eat. Raptors have such keen eyesight, they can spot a small animal on the ground far below. With sharp claws called talons, they grasp the animal and carry it away.

Many raptors migrate, or move from one area to another, twice a year. These birds must move to a warmer climate when winter comes because the small animals they eat are hidden under the snow. In the spring, they return north. There they will raise their young.

7. What are raptors?

_____

8. What is a talon?

_____

9. Why do raptors move to a warmer climate when winter comes?

_____

10. What does the word *migrate* mean?

_____

11. When do raptors return north?

_____

12. Where do raptors raise their young?

_____

READING FOR DETAILS

 **DIRECTIONS:**

Read the steps below.

> To Recall Specific Facts and Details:
> 1. READ the story carefully.
> 2. READ the question carefully.
> 3. THINK about what the question is asking.
> 4. REREAD the story if necessary to answer the question.

Read the selection to yourself. Choose the correct answer to complete each sentence. Fill in the answer circle in front of your answer.

Did you know that all brown bears are not brown? The name "brown bear" includes kinds of bears from North America, Europe, and Asia. Some brown bears have gray, tan, or even blond hair. No matter what their color, brown bears all have rounded faces and humps on their backs. The Alaskan brown bear is one of the world's largest meat-eating land animals. An adult Alaskan brown bear can weigh as much as 1,700 pounds, about the same as a small car. The grizzly bear also belongs to the family of brown bears. A grizzly isn't as big as the Alaskan brown bear, and lives in other areas such as Alaska, western Canada, and in small areas of Wyoming, Montana, and Idaho.

1. All brown bears ____.
   ⓐ can weigh as much as 1,700 pounds
   ⓑ live in Wyoming, Montana, and Idaho
   ⓒ are the world's largest meat-eating land animals
   ⓓ have rounded faces and humps on their backs

2. The Alaskan brown bear ____.
   ⓐ is one of the world's largest meat-eating land animals
   ⓑ lives in small areas of Wyoming, Montana, and Idaho
   ⓒ isn't related to the grizzly bear
   ⓓ is smaller than a grizzly bear

Go on to the next page.

Name _____   Date _____

READING FOR DETAILS (P. 2)

DIRECTIONS:

Read the selection to yourself. Choose the correct answer for each question. Fill in the answer circle in front of your answer.

Silver is a metal that has been treasured for over 5,000 years. People have dug up nearly a million tons of silver over that period of time. Much of this silver has been used to make coins. Some historians think that the first silver coins were made between 600 B.C. and 500 B.C. Silver has been shaped into other objects as well, including jewelry, cups, and bowls.

Silver reflects light better than any other substance. Pure silver is malleable. That means that it can be pounded or beaten into shapes without its breaking. Silver can be pounded into sheets that are thinner than paper. Very few things are made of pure silver today. Often other metals are mixed with silver to make it harder. Coins that once contained silver, such as dimes and quarters, are now made completely of nickel and copper.

3. How many years has silver been treasured?
   ⓐ one million
   ⓑ 500
   ⓒ 600
   ⓓ 5,000

4. What does the word *malleable* mean?
   ⓐ materials that are used to make coins
   ⓑ materials that are made completely of nickel and copper
   ⓒ materials that can be pounded or beaten without breaking
   ⓓ materials that are mixed with silver

5. What are coins such as dimes and quarters now made of?
   ⓐ pure silver
   ⓑ nickel and copper
   ⓒ silver mixed with other metals
   ⓓ malleable metals

Facts

Name _____ Date _____

FACT FINDING

 **DIRECTIONS:**

Read the selection to yourself. Choose the correct answer to complete each sentence. Fill in the answer circle in front of your answer.

The human body reacts when there are changes in the temperature. In hot weather, there are two types of emergencies that may occur because of the heat. They are heat exhaustion and heat stroke. Heat exhaustion may happen to someone in an overheated room. The body reacts by sweating or causing the person's face to become pale. Some people may vomit. Anyone with heat exhaustion should be placed in a cool, shady spot. The person's feet should be raised, and clothing loosened. Give the person sips of water, if possible, and apply cool, wet cloths to the forehead.

Heat stroke is much more serious than heat exhaustion. Heat stroke is usually caused by staying, or working, in the sun for too long. If heat stroke is suspected, a doctor should be called at once. The face of a person with heat stroke becomes very hot, red, and dry. Breathing becomes slow and noisy, and the pulse becomes fast and strong. The person may pass out. Move the person to a cool, shaded spot. If possible, raise the person's head, and apply cool, wet cloths. Remove all outer clothing. If the person has not passed out, small sips of water can be given.

1. _____ of a person with heat exhaustion.
   ⓐ Raise the head
   ⓑ Raise the feet
   ⓒ Shake the hand
   ⓓ Touch the skin

2. A person with heat stroke _____.
   ⓐ will have a fast and strong pulse
   ⓑ should be given a glass of lemonade
   ⓒ will have cold sweat on the forehead
   ⓓ has usually been in an overheated room

3. People with heat exhaustion or heat stroke are alike in that they both ___.
   ⓐ need immediate attention from a doctor
   ⓑ should lie on their back with their head raised
   ⓒ should be taken to a cool, shady place
   ⓓ have slow and noisy breathing

Go on to the next page.

FACT FINDING (P. 2)

DIRECTIONS: Read the selection to yourself. Choose the correct answer for each question. Fill in the circle in front of your answer.

The California condor is one of the largest and rarest birds on Earth. An adult can grow to be about four feet long and weigh about twenty pounds. When its wings are stretched, they can measure about nine feet from wingtip to wingtip. Two hundred years ago, hundreds and hundreds of California condors lived along the Pacific coast from Canada to Mexico. Today there may be fewer than twenty-five of the birds alive.

No one is sure what is causing the birds to die out. Some scientists are trying very hard to save the birds. Usually, the females only lay one egg every two years. However, some studies have shown that when an egg is taken from the nest, many condors lay a new egg to replace it. Some scientists are removing eggs and trying to hatch the eggs in an incubator. That is one of the ways scientists are trying to save the California condor.

4. About how many California condors are believed to be alive today?
   ⓐ two
   ⓑ four
   ⓒ nine
   ⓓ twenty-five

5. How often does a female California condor normally lay an egg?
   ⓐ once a year
   ⓑ once every two years
   ⓒ once every four years
   ⓓ once every six years

Facts

Name_____ Date_____

THE ORDER OF EVENTS

**DIRECTIONS:**

Read the following passage and think about the order in which the events occurred.

Charlie's mother was coming home from the hospital this afternoon. Charlie wanted to clean the house before she got home. **First** he swept all the floors. **Next** he dusted the furniture. **Then** he mopped the kitchen floor. The **last** thing he had to do was wash the dishes and put them away.

The above passage has clue words that help you keep track of the order of events. Sometimes authors give you these clues to make it clearer when things happened. Some authors do not give you clue words. Then you must try to separate the events and keep track of their order without the clues. Read the following passage. It is the same story without clue words.

Charlie's mother was coming home from the hospital this afternoon. Charlie wanted to clean the house before she got home. He swept all the floors. He dusted the furniture. He mopped the kitchen floor. He washed the dishes and put them away.

Sometimes it is important to get the sequence, or order of events, in mind so that you can better understand the story.

To Arrange Events in Order:
1. READ the story carefully.
2. LOOK to see if there are clue words.
3. FIND each event.
4. DECIDE in what order the events happen.

Now read this passage. Number the events in the order they happened.

Janet had called and asked Vicki if she wanted to go swimming. Vicki put on her swimming suit. She got her towel and sunglasses. She put some new batteries in her radio. She put everything in her beach bag. When she looked out the window to see if Janet was coming, she saw that it was raining!

a._____ Vicki put new batteries in her radio.
b._____ Vicki got her towel and sunglasses.
c._____ Vicki put everything in her beach bag.
d._____ Vicki looked out the window.
e._____ Janet called Vicki.
f._____ Vicki put on her swimsuit.

Sequence

© Steck-Vaughn Company   75   Study Skills 4, SV 8052-9

Name _____   Date _____

WHAT HAPPENED NEXT?

DIRECTIONS:

Read each passage. Number the events in the order that they happened.

Bill was trying to save enough money to buy a football helmet. He had saved twenty dollars, but he still needed fifteen more. Bill earned five dollars by cleaning his grandmother's garage. He earned three dollars by giving his neighbor's dog a bath. Bill weeded his mother's garden for two dollars. He cut his aunt's grass for three dollars. His father let him wash the car for two more dollars. Finally, he had the money. He went to the sporting goods store and bought his helmet.

1. a. ____ Bill gave his neighbor's dog a bath.
    b. ____ Bill washed his father's car.
    c. ____ Bill saved twenty dollars.
    d. ____ Bill cleaned his grandmother's garage.
    e. ____ Bill weeded his mother's garden.
    f. ____ Bill bought his helmet.
    g. ____ Bill mowed his aunt's grass.

Everything had gone just as planned. As soon as the bell rang, the students sat in their seats. Ms. Clark had no idea that something special was about to happen. Lisa Miller asked for permission to be excused. Ms. Clark said she could. When Lisa came back in, she was carrying a birthday cake with candles on it. The class started singing "Happy Birthday." Ms. Clark was very surprised. Tommy Adams got some plates and forks from a sack in his locker. Everyone enjoyed a piece of the birthday cake.

2. a. ____ Ms. Clark said Lisa could be excused.
    b. ____ Tommy got some plates and forks.
    c. ____ The school bell rang.
    d. ____ Ms. Clark was very surprised.
    e. ____ Lisa Miller asked to be excused.
    f. ____ The class started singing "Happy Birthday."
    g. ____ Lisa brought in a birthday cake.

Sequence

Name _____   Date _____

REMEMBERING SEQUENCE

DIRECTIONS:

Read the following passage. Then answer the questions.

The darkling beetle has an interesting way to keep from freezing in the winter. After the beetle hatches from its egg, it turns into a wormlike larva. In the fall, the larva finds shelter in a log. There it starts making a protein that acts as an antifreeze inside its body. When winter comes, the larva keeps warm by using its antifreeze and the shelter of the log. In the spring, the larva becomes active. It changes into a pupa. Then it becomes an adult beetle.

1. What does the beetle turn into after it hatches from the egg?

_____

2. What does the beetle do just before it starts making a protein inside its body?

_____

3. What happens to the beetle during the winter?

_____

4. What happens to the beetle just before it changes into a pupa?

_____

5. What happens to the beetle just after the pupa stage?

_____

Name _____ Date _____

THE RIGHT ORDER

 **DIRECTIONS:**

Read the following recipe. Then answer the questions.

Pumpkin Bread

1 3/4 cups of flour
1 teaspoon baking soda
1/2 teaspoon salt
1 1/2 cups of sugar
1/2 teaspoon nutmeg

1/2 teaspoon cinnamon
1/2 cup water
1/2 cup cooking oil
2 eggs
1 cup of canned pumpkin

Preheat the oven to 350°. Grease a loaf pan with shortening. In a large bowl mix the flour, baking soda, salt, sugar, nutmeg, and cinnamon. Stir in the water and cooking oil. Beat in the eggs. Add the pumpkin. Stir the mixture until the ingredients are blended. Pour the mixture into the pan. Bake for one hour. Let the bread cool before removing it from the pan.

1. What do you do <u>first</u>?
_____

2. What do you do <u>just after</u> you grease the loaf pan?
_____

3. What do you do <u>just before</u> you beat in the eggs?
_____

4. What do you do <u>just after</u> you add the pumpkin?
_____

5. What do you do <u>just after</u> you pour the mixture into the pan?
_____

6. What do you do <u>last</u>?
_____

Name _____ Date _____

WHAT HAPPENED WHEN?

Read the steps below.

> **To Identify the Order of Events:**
> 1. READ the story carefully.
> 2. LOOK to see if there are clue words.
> 3. FIND each event.
> 4. DECIDE in what order the events happen.

Read each selection to yourself. Choose the correct answer to each question. Fill in the answer circle in front of your answer.

    Justin crawled into his bed. He was very tired. His day had been very busy. First, he had gone fishing with his dad. They had caught enough fish for dinner. When they got home, he and his dad had cleaned the fish. Then they ate lunch. After lunch he had gone to baseball practice. The coach had really given them a workout! When he got home, he and his father cooked the fish they had caught that morning. Then they had supper, and Justin washed the dishes. As soon as the dishes were washed, he had gone to a movie with his mother and father. It had been a great day, but also a very busy one!

1. What did Justin do <u>right after</u> he helped clean the fish?
   - ⓐ went to baseball practice
   - ⓑ went to a movie
   - ⓒ ate lunch
   - ⓓ washed the dishes

2. What did Justin do <u>just before</u> he went to a movie?
   - ⓐ went fishing
   - ⓑ went to baseball practice
   - ⓒ washed the dishes
   - ⓓ ate lunch

Go on to the next page.

Sequence

Name _____ Date _____

WHAT HAPPENED WHEN? (P. 2)

DIRECTIONS:

Read each selection to yourself. Choose the correct answer to each question. Fill in the answer circle in front of your answers.

The water we drink comes from rivers and lakes. This fresh water must be purified before it is safe for drinking. Pipes take the water to a water-treatment plant. There it goes through several steps that clean the water before it is used by humans. First, the water is sprayed into the air so that it mixes with oxygen. The oxygen helps bacteria to grow, and the bacteria eat impurities. After a chemical called alum is added, the water swirls through a large mixing tank. The alum forms sticky particles. Dirt and other impurities stick to these particles. Next, the water flows into a settling tank where the particles sink to the bottom. Then the water flows into a filter tank. In the tank are layers of charcoal, sand, gravel, and rocks. These filters catch any particles remaining in the water. Finally, a chemical called chlorine is added. This chemical kills any germs that can cause diseases. At this point, the water is clean and ready to be pumped to where it will be used.

3. What is the <u>first</u> step in cleaning water?
   - ⓐ pouring it into a filter tank
   - ⓑ the water is sprayed into the air
   - ⓒ chlorine is added
   - ⓓ alum is added

4. What happens to the water <u>just after</u> alum is added?
   - ⓐ the water swirls through a large mixing tank
   - ⓑ the water is sprayed through the air
   - ⓒ the water is put through a filter tank
   - ⓓ chlorine is added

5. What happens to the water <u>just before</u> chlorine is added?
   - ⓐ alum is added
   - ⓑ the water is poured through a filter tank
   - ⓒ the water is sprayed into the air
   - ⓓ the water swirls through a large mixing tank

Sequence

Name _____ Date _____

WHAT DO YOU DO?

DIRECTIONS:

Read the recipe for gingerbread boy cookies. Choose the correct answer to each question. Fill in the answer circle in front of your answer.

Gingerbread Boy Cookies

1/3 cup soft shortening	1 tsp. salt
1 cup brown sugar	1 tsp. allspice
1 1/2 cups dark molasses	1 tsp. ginger
2/3 cup cold water	1 tsp. cloves
7 cups flour	1 tsp. cinnamon
2 tsp. soda	1 cup raisins

Mix shortening, brown sugar, and molasses. Stir in water. Blend flour, soda, and spices together. Stir in with other ingredients. Chill dough for one hour. Heat oven to 350 degrees. Lightly grease a baking sheet. Roll dough 1/2 inch thick. Cut with floured gingerbread boy cookie cutter. Place cookies on baking sheet. Add raisins for eyes and mouth. Bake 10 to 12 minutes. Cool slightly, then carefully remove from baking sheet.

1. What do you do <u>just after</u> you mix the shortening, brown sugar, and molasses?
   ⓐ chill dough for one hour
   ⓑ add raisins for eyes and mouth
   ⓒ heat oven to 350 degrees
   ⓓ stir in water

2. What do you do <u>just before</u> you grease a baking sheet?
   ⓐ chill dough for one hour
   ⓑ heat oven to 350 degrees
   ⓒ roll dough 1/2 inch thick
   ⓓ blend flour, soda, and spices

3. What do you do <u>just before</u> you add the raisins for the eyes and mouth?
   ⓐ place cookies on baking sheet
   ⓑ heat oven to 350 degrees
   ⓒ chill dough for one hour
   ⓓ roll dough 1/2 inch thick

Go on to the next page.

Sequence

Name _____ Date _____

WHAT DO YOU DO? (P. 2)

DIRECTIONS:

Read the directions for cleaning your room. Choose the correct answer to each question. Fill in the answer circle in front of your answer.

How to Clean Your Room

Dust cloth   **Vacuum or broom**
Furniture polish   **Wastebasket**

Stand in the doorway, and take a good look at your room. Picture in your mind where everything should be. Then, gather all the cleaning materials you will need.

First, make up your bed. Then pick up everything that is on the floor. Hang your clothes in the closet. Fold any clothes that should be placed in drawers or boxes. Place dirty clothes in a pile outside your doorway. Put your toys in a box or chest. Next, vacuum or sweep the floor. Spray polish on the dust cloth, and dust the furniture. Finally, stand outside your doorway and admire your beautiful room! Pick up the dirty clothes in the hallway and put them with the family's dirty laundry.

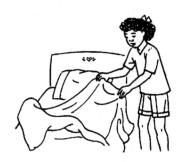

4. What do you do <u>just before</u> you dust the furniture?
   ⓐ Hang your clothes in the closet.
   ⓑ Spray polish on the dust cloth.
   ⓒ Vacuum or sweep the floor.
   ⓓ Gather all cleaning materials.

5. What do you do <u>just after</u> you hang your clothes in the closet?
   ⓐ Picture in your mind where everything should be.
   ⓑ Pick up everything that is on the floor.
   ⓒ Fold other clothes and place them in drawers or boxes.
   ⓓ Stand in the hallway and admire your beautiful room!

Sequence

Name _____ Date _____

WRAPPING IT UP

 **DIRECTIONS:**

Read this story and think about how you would tell the main idea and important events in a few sentences.

It was Tina's first day at her new school. She was very nervous. She didn't know anyone. Her new teacher was nice and asked another girl, Linda, to help Tina through her first day. At recess, Linda and her friends played with Tina. Tina knew she would like her new school.

Before you can retell this story in a few sentences, you must decide what the important parts of the story are. For this story you would probably say:

Tina was nervous the first day at her new school. Soon she made friends and knew that she would like it there.

When you tell a short form of a story, you are making a summary. A summary is a short account of the main idea and important details. There are some things that you leave out of a summary. That is because they are less important than the main idea and important details.

> **To Summarize a Story:**
> 1. **READ** the story carefully.
> 2. **THINK** about its main idea and important details.
> 3. **INCLUDE** only those ideas in your summary.

Now read these selections and write a summary. Use complete sentences.

Charles and his friends went fishing all afternoon. Mike caught two fish. Pat caught three. John caught five. Charles only caught one, but it was the biggest.

1. _____
   _____

Charlotte stayed at Nicole's house. Nicole's parents let them stay up and watch a scary movie on television. That night, they had trouble falling asleep. They kept thinking about the monster in the movie.

2. _____
   _____

Name _____   Date _____

THE MAIN IDEA AND A LITTLE MORE

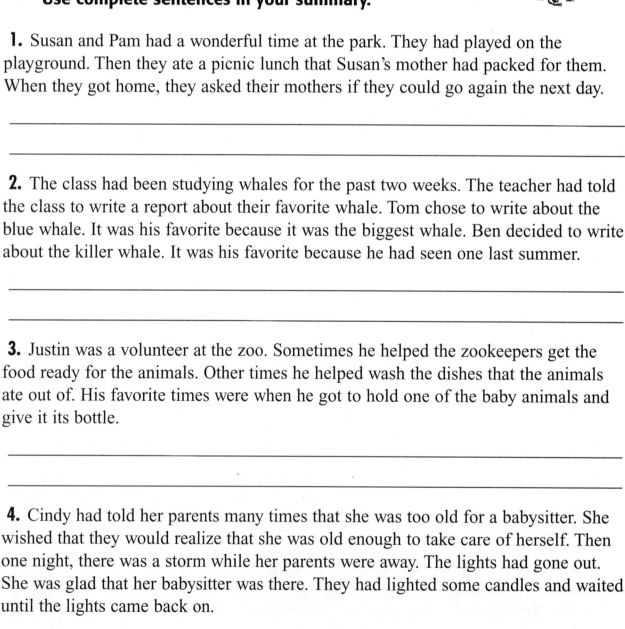

DIRECTIONS:

Read each story and write a summary of each. Use complete sentences in your summary.

1. Susan and Pam had a wonderful time at the park. They had played on the playground. Then they ate a picnic lunch that Susan's mother had packed for them. When they got home, they asked their mothers if they could go again the next day.

_____

_____

2. The class had been studying whales for the past two weeks. The teacher had told the class to write a report about their favorite whale. Tom chose to write about the blue whale. It was his favorite because it was the biggest whale. Ben decided to write about the killer whale. It was his favorite because he had seen one last summer.

_____

_____

3. Justin was a volunteer at the zoo. Sometimes he helped the zookeepers get the food ready for the animals. Other times he helped wash the dishes that the animals ate out of. His favorite times were when he got to hold one of the baby animals and give it its bottle.

_____

_____

4. Cindy had told her parents many times that she was too old for a babysitter. She wished that they would realize that she was old enough to take care of herself. Then one night, there was a storm while her parents were away. The lights had gone out. She was glad that her babysitter was there. They had lighted some candles and waited until the lights came back on.

_____

_____

Name _____ Date _____

IN SUMMARY

DIRECTIONS:

Read each story. Then read the answer choices. Decide which one is the best summary of the story. Fill in the answer circle in front of your answer.

As Melissa got ready for the first day of school, she thought about all that had happened that summer. She had broken her leg early in June. It had seemed as if the summer was going to be ruined because she couldn't go swimming. Then she had started going to the Girls' Club, which had cooking and craft centers, as well as a swimming pool. She had a wonderful time and had learned to make many new things.

1. Which of the following is the best summary of the above story?
ⓐ Melissa had spent most of the winter at the Girls' Club.
ⓑ Even though Melissa broke her leg, she had a good summer.
ⓒ Melissa broke her leg early in the summer.
ⓓ Melissa got ready for the first day of school.

Steve had worked very hard on his exhibit for the fair. He was going to enter the photography contest. He had taken over a hundred pictures during the summer. It had been hard to choose only twenty of them to put in the contest. Once he had done that, he had to glue them carefully and neatly on some poster board. All his work paid off when he won first prize.

2. Which of the following is the best summary of the above story?
ⓐ Steve had a hard time choosing what pictures to enter.
ⓑ Steve carefully glued his pictures on poster board.
ⓒ Steve took over a hundred pictures during the summer.
ⓓ Steve's hard work paid off when he won first prize.

After Jim crawled into his tent, he had a hard time falling asleep. There seemed to be a hundred rocks right under his sleeping bag. He was able to shift some of the large ones to the side. He knew he would have to move more of the rocks tomorrow. He finally fell asleep listening to the sounds of the woods.

3. Which of the following is the best summary of the above story?
ⓐ Jim wasn't very comfortable, but finally fell asleep.
ⓑ Jim knew he should move some of the rocks.
ⓒ Jim shifted some of the large rocks to the side.
ⓓ Jim liked to listen to the sounds of the woods.

Go on to the next page.

Name _____   Date _____

IN SUMMARY (P. 2)

DIRECTIONS: Read each story. Then read the answer choices. Decide which one is the best summary of the story. Fill in the answer circle in front of your answer.

Maria decided to make a cake. She started to get everything ready. Just then the phone rang. It was her friend Gail. They started talking. Before Maria knew it, she had been talking for over an hour! She said good-bye to Gail and went into the kitchen. She wanted to have the cake finished for her father before he got home.

4. Which of the following is the best summary of the above story?
ⓐ Maria talked to her friend for over one hour.
ⓑ Maria was making a cake for her father's birthday.
ⓒ Maria talked for so long, she had to hurry to make the cake.
ⓓ Maria's friend Gail called her on the telephone.

Jamie's uncle came to visit. Jamie took his uncle up to his room. Jamie wanted to show his uncle the new coins he had in his coin collection. He had gotten three new coins since his uncle last visited. He had a 1921 penny and a 1932 nickel. His favorite new coin was a 1902 dime.

5. Which of the following is the best summary of the above story?
ⓐ Jamie's favorite coin was a 1902 dime.
ⓑ Jamie had just gotten three new coins.
ⓒ Jamie showed his uncle his new coins.
ⓓ Jamie's uncle came to visit him.

Cindy's cousin called and asked her to spend the weekend at his house. Cindy liked to go to her cousin's house. They always had lots of fun together. Cindy had a big school project due on Monday. She had most of the things she needed, but she knew it would take her a while to put it all together. She told her cousin that maybe she could come over next weekend.

6. Which of the following is the best summary of the above story?
ⓐ Cindy always had fun at her cousin's house.
ⓑ Cindy told her cousin she would visit this weekend.
ⓒ Cindy had homework, so she didn't go to her cousin's.
ⓓ Cindy had a big school project due on Monday.

Name _____ Date _____

CONCLUSIONS

 **Directions:**

Read the following story and think about its meaning.

Tom heard a loud noise upstairs. He ran up the steps. His little brother was holding the cord to the lamp in their mother's room. The lamp was on the floor.

What is happening in this story? You could conclude that Tom's little brother had pulled the lamp down. Sometimes an author may not tell you directly what is happening. You may have to make a conclusion based on the facts from the story and your own experiences.

Sometimes when you are reading a story your conclusion may not be correct. When this happens, you can always change your conclusion based on new information from the story.

> **To Draw Conclusions:**
> 1. **READ** the story carefully.
> 2. **THINK** about the facts in the story and your own past experiences.
> 3. **DECIDE** what has happened in the story.

Read the following stories and draw a conclusion for each. Write your conclusion on the line in a complete sentence.

Harry came in the house. He took off his shorts and put on some long pants. Then he got a jacket out of his closet. He went back outside to play.

1. What can you conclude about what is happening outside?

_____

_____

Betty put on her pajamas and brushed her teeth. She went downstairs to say goodnight to her parents.

2. What can you conclude about what Betty is doing?

_____

_____

Conclusion

Name _____ Date _____

WHAT CAN YOU CONCLUDE?

DIRECTIONS:

Read the following stories and draw a conclusion for each. Write your conclusion on the line in a complete sentence.

Ms. Thomas passed back the math test. Paul looked unhappy but Karen had a big smile on her face.

1. What can you conclude about Paul and Karen?

_____
_____

Steve looked at the place where his house once stood. The smell of smoke was still heavy in the air. He and his family were just glad that no one was home when the fire had started.

2. What can you conclude about Steve's house?

_____
_____

Vicki was sorry for what she had said to Bob. Bob was her best friend. She didn't know why he had gotten so upset! She called Bob on the telephone to say that she was sorry.

3. What can you conclude about Vicki and Bob?

_____
_____

Jennifer said good-bye to her friends. She went back into the living room and looked at all her presents. She was going to take them up to her room after she ate the last piece of cake.

4. What can you conclude about what has happened at Jennifer's house?

_____
_____

Conclusion

Name _____ Date _____

DRAWING CONCLUSIONS

DIRECTIONS:

Read the following stories and draw a conclusion for each. Write your conclusion on the line in a complete sentence.

Karen was able to get out of bed and pack her things. She was feeling much better. She thought back on how scared she had been the day she had come. It wasn't nearly as bad as she had thought it would be. She had made friends with several of the nurses and Tina, the girl who was sharing her room. Tina's doctor had told her she could go home tomorrow.

1. What can you conclude about Karen?
_____
_____

Tim thought this was the only bad part. He helped his father put the tent and lantern away in the garage. He carried the bags of dirty clothes to the basement. He started washing all the dirty dishes.

2. What can you conclude about what Tim is doing?
_____
_____

Diane kept looking out the window. Her parents should have been home two hours ago. She was very worried about them. They usually called when they were going to be this late. Suddenly Diane smiled and ran to the door.

3. What can you conclude about why Diane ran to the door?
_____
_____

Carla and her mother were both carrying lots of bags and packages. They couldn't believe Aunt Sarah wanted to go to another store.

4. What can you conclude about what Carla has been doing?
_____
_____

Go on to the next page.

Name _____   Date _____

DRAWING CONCLUSIONS (P. 2)

DIRECTIONS:

Read the following stories and draw a conclusion for each. Write your conclusion on the line in a complete sentence.

Tom's friends signed their names on his cast. He was finally getting used to it. He could walk pretty well now. One thing he knew for sure, he would be more careful on his bike from now on.

5. What can you conclude about what happened to Tom?

_____
_____

Everything seemed different around the house since Eddie's mother had come home from the hospital. It seemed like the telephone hadn't stopped ringing, and several of Eddie's relatives had visited during the past few days. There were bottles all around the kitchen, and tiny little clothes and diapers everywhere that people had brought over as gifts.

6. What can you conclude about what has happened at Eddie's house?

_____
_____

It had already been a great day. Jessica and her family had gone to the parade that morning. They spent the afternoon at the beach swimming. Then they had a picnic. But the best part was yet to come. At dusk, they were going to light sparklers and then go to watch the fireworks.

7. What can you conclude about what day this story takes place on?

_____
_____

The leaves were starting to turn orange and red. The days were becoming cooler and shorter. Hank put on his jacket and got ready to go to the football game.

8. What can you conclude about what time of the year it is?

_____
_____

Conclusion

Name _____ Date _____

AND YOUR CONCLUSION IS

Read the steps below.

> **To Draw Conclusions:**
> 1. READ the story carefully.
> 2. THINK about the facts in the story and your past experiences.
> 3. DECIDE what has happened in the story.

Read each selection to yourself. Choose the correct answer to each question. Fill in the answer circle in front of your answer.

Terry's mother was in the kitchen cooking supper. She asked Terry to go next door and borrow two eggs from Mrs. Hampton. She told him to hurry.

1. What can you conclude from this story?
ⓐ Mrs. Hampton has borrowed eggs from Terry's mother.
ⓑ Terry's mother needs two eggs for what she is cooking.
ⓒ Terry's mother is baking a cake.
ⓓ Terry loves to eat fried eggs.

Nadine sat in the chair and opened her mouth as wide as she could. The dentist found the tooth with the hole, and started the drill. She couldn't feel anything since the dentist had given her a shot to numb her mouth.

2. What can you conclude is happening in this story?
ⓐ Nadine doesn't like the dentist.
ⓑ Nadine wanted more holes in her teeth.
ⓒ Nadine is getting a cavity filled.
ⓓ Nadine likes to brush her teeth.

Go on to the next page.

Name _____   Date _____

AND YOUR CONCLUSION IS (P. 2)

DIRECTIONS:

Read each selection to yourself. Choose the correct answer to each question. Fill in the answer circle in front of your answer.

The scout troop decided to take a rest. They found a shady spot near the lake. They put down their backpacks and had a drink of water. They talked about the trees, birds, and flowers they had seen along the way.

3. What can you conclude from this story?
  ⓐ The scout troop is lost.
  ⓑ The scout troop hasn't rested all week.
  ⓒ The scout troop is taking a hike.
  ⓓ The scout troop is on their way home.

Steve had looked everywhere he could think of. He decided to go home and make some signs. He wrote his phone number and what his dog looked like on the signs. He put the signs around his neighborhood. He went home hoping to get a phone call soon.

4. What can you conclude from this story?
  ⓐ Steve has lost his dog.
  ⓑ Steve likes to make signs.
  ⓒ Steve hopes his friend Mike will call.
  ⓓ Steve's dog is wearing a collar.

Diane hung up the phone and went to the garage. She got Susan's bike and rode it over to Susan's house. She didn't blame Susan for getting angry. Susan had been nice enough to let Diane use the bike for her paper route. Diane knew she should have returned the bike yesterday, like she had promised.

5. What can you conclude from this story?
  ⓐ Diane and Susan often argue.
  ⓑ Diane needs a new garage.
  ⓒ Susan let Diane borrow her bike.
  ⓓ Susan never returns things she borrows.

Name _____ Date _____

IN CONCLUSION

Read each selection to yourself. Choose the correct answer to each question. Fill in the answer circle in front of your answer.

Mindy had a hard time falling asleep. She wasn't used to hearing so much traffic at night. She lived in the country and usually heard nothing but crickets on a summer night. She looked at her cousin Beth lying in the bed next to hers. She was looking forward to tomorrow when Beth would show her around her neighborhood.

1. What can you conclude from this story?
   ⓐ Mindy and her cousin haven't seen each other for years.
   ⓑ Mindy always has trouble sleeping when she isn't home.
   ⓒ Mindy is visiting her cousin in the city.
   ⓓ Mindy has never been to such a large country.

Kyle hung his head as he walked down the hall toward the principal's office. He was ashamed of what he had done. He didn't blame his teacher for sending him to see the principal. He just hoped the principal wouldn't call his parents. They would be very disappointed in him.

2. What can you conclude from this story?
   ⓐ Kyle broke a window in his classroom.
   ⓑ Kyle has never been in trouble before.
   ⓒ Kyle has done something wrong.
   ⓓ Kyle doesn't think his teacher was fair.

Doug counted his money one more time. He had been counting his money every week for a month. He finally had enough money. He went downstairs and asked his mother when she could take him to get his new tennis racket.

3. What can you conclude from this story?
   ⓐ Doug has been saving his money for a new tennis racket.
   ⓑ Doug gets three dollars a week for his allowance.
   ⓒ Doug is an excellent tennis player.
   ⓓ Doug has mowed lawns to earn money.

Go on to the next page.

Name _____ Date _____

IN CONCLUSION (P. 2)

Read each selection to yourself. Choose the correct answer to each question. Fill in the answer circle in front of your answer.

Donna walked into the doctor's office. She said hello to Ms. Clayton, the nurse sitting at the desk. The nurse wrote Donna's name on a sheet of paper and told Donna she shouldn't have to wait very long to get her allergy shot. Donna sat on a chair and started reading a magazine.

4. What can you conclude from this story?
   ⓐ Donna is allergic to dust and mold.
   ⓑ Donna has been to this doctor's office before.
   ⓒ Donna will be late for school.
   ⓓ Donna has had allergies since she was two.

As Lyle looked over his math test the teacher had just returned, he knew he should have studied. The night before the test he had played outside all evening and then watched television. He knew he would have to work extra hard in math to make up for the grade he got on this test.

5. What can you conclude from this story?
   ⓐ Lyle is usually a straight-A student.
   ⓑ Lyle's favorite subject is math.
   ⓒ Lyle never studies for tests.
   ⓓ Lyle received a poor grade on the test.

Conclusion

Study Skills for Fourth Grade
Answer Key

Pp.6-8 Assessment
1. Star next to name, circle around star, square around page number.
2. a. D b. C
3. measure
4. a. 100 b. 4
5. a. title page b. table of contents c. glossary d. index
6. Answers will vary: excited, happy
7. a. 4 b. 1 c. 6 d. 3 e. 2 f. 5
8. Answers may vary: a. playground, park b. later afternoon, suppertime, evening
9. a. realistic b. fantasy c. historical
10. a. figurative b. literal c. figurative d. literal
11. a. fact b. opinion c. fact d. opinion
12. a. underline Bob didn't go; circle he had homework b. underline the game was called off; circle as a result of the rain
13. Cindy will write a letter to Katie.
14. B
15. Charles and his friends went fishing.

P. 9 Picture should resemble a house and include all elements listed in directions.

P. 10 Picture should resemble a pig and include all elements listed in directions.

P. 11
1. bait
2. scary

P. 12
1. e
2. k
3. b
4. m
5. p
6. d
7. i
8. l
9. f
10. a
11. o
12. c
13. j
14. h
15. n
16. g

P. 13
1. A
2. C
3. A
4. A
5. D
6. B
7. B
8. D
9. B
10. C

P. 14 Answers will vary.
1. a disguise
2. to show clearly
3. to change the usual appearance to conceal the true identity
4. a framework of thin strips to form a network
5. ugly in disposition or temper
6. the real or essential nature
7. the real part of something

P. 15 Answers will vary.
1. to check of defeat by confusing
2. a bad or stupid mistake
3. in a natural state
4. nobleness, worthiness
5. outer, external
6. to move or act in a lazy way

P. 16
meal, mechanics, maze, mean, mayor, measure, meant

P. 17
1. 2
2. 6
3. 7
4. 1
5. 4
6. 6
7. 3
8. 4
9. 7
10. 3

P. 18
1. a. 70 b. 8
2. a.100 b. 4
3. a. 1 b. 6
4. a. 95 b. 95

P. 19
1.-3. Order will vary; Bowwow, Collie, Puppy
4.-6. Order will vary; Rover, Dog, Poodle
7. Poodle Parkway
8.-9. Order will vary; Bowwow and Rover
10. Dog Drive

P. 20
1. D
2. B
3. D
4. B

P. 21
1. A
2. D
3. B
4. D

P. 22
1. D
2. C
3. C

P. 23
1. glossary
2. index
3. index
4. glossary
5. index
6. glossary
7. index
8. glossary

P. 24
1. 145
2. 15
3. 129
4. 20
5. 143
6. 24
7. 141
8. 133
9. 23
10. 18

P. 25
1. cambium
2. arbor
3. deciduous
4. pith
5. coniferous
6. botany

P. 26
1. A
2. D
3. B
4. C
5. D
6. C
7. D
8. A
9. B
10. A

P. 28 Answers will vary.
1. Charles was very determined.
2. Charles has a strong will.
3. happy, glad
4. sad, unhappy

P. 29
1. Nick
2. the teacher and Karen

Answers will vary.
3. Nick was very honest.
4. He wanted to see how well he could do on the test by himself.
5. Nick felt proud.
6. It is better to be honest.

P. 30 Answers will vary.
1. afraid, scared
2. sorry, sad
3. excited, happy, proud
4. upset, angry
5. excited, happy
6. upset, angry

P. 31
a. 4
b. 6
c. 9
d. 1
e. 2
f. 5
g. 7
h. 8
i. 3

P. 32
a. 9
b. 4
c. 11
d. 5
e. 1
f. 8
g. 6
h. 7
i. 2
j. 3
k. 10
l. 12

P. 33 Answers will vary.
1. campground, lake
2. morning, summer
3. school
4. winter, morning

P. 34
1. Barry's house
2. New Year's Eve, night
3. Grandparent's house, farm
4. evening, night
5. playground, park
6. late afternoon, suppertime, evening
7. planet Xmpet
8. year 8437
9. car, country, road
10. noon, lunchtime, fall

P. 35
1. fantasy
2. historical
3. realistic
4. realistic
5. fantasy
6. historical

P. 36
1. historical
2. realistic
3. realistic
4. fantasy
5. fantasy
6. historical
7. fantasy
8. realistic
9. historical
10. fantasy

P. 37
1. figurative
2. literal
3. literal
4. figurative
5. figurative
6. literal
7. figurative
8. literal
9. figurative
10. literal

P. 38 Answers will vary.
1. John had been swimming for a long time.
2. Mother carries many things in her purse.
3. Tom speaks loudly.
4. Elsie swims very well.
5. Carl wasn't thinking when he said that.
6. People on the ground seemed smaller as the plane went higher.
7. The man was very slender.
8. Bob is hard to awaken.
9. Karen was getting very hot from the heat.
10. I was very frightened when Doug scared me.

P. 39
1. nonfiction
2. nonfiction
3. fiction

Pp. 40–41
1. fiction
2. nonfiction
3. nonfiction
4. nonfiction
5. fiction
6. nonfiction
7. nonfiction
8. fiction
9. fiction
10. fiction
11. nonfiction
12. fiction
13. nonfiction
14. nonfiction
15. nonfiction
16. nonfiction

17. fiction
18. fiction
Pp. 40–41 (cont.)
19. nonfiction
20. nonfiction
21. nonfiction
22. nonfiction
23. fiction
24. nonfiction
25. fiction
26. nonfiction
27. nonfiction
28. fiction
P. 42 Answers will vary.
Pp. 43–44
1. D
2. B
3. C
4. D
5. A
Pp. 45–46
1. A
2. B
3. B
4. C
5. A
6. A
Pp. 47–48
1. Bob didn't go (effect) because he had homework and he was tired (causes).
2. The game was called off (effect) as a result of the cold and rain (causes).
3. Tim was saving his money (effect) since he wanted to buy a new ball and a new bat (causes).
David was very hungry.
4. David had not eaten breakfast.
5. He had been playing very hard.
Martha did very well on the history test.
6. She had read the chapter twice.
7. Her mother asked her questions.
His parents gave him $7.00 for his work.
8. Robert had cleaned the garage.
9. He had raked the leaves.
Pp. 49–50
Eddie was very happy when his parents agreed to go camping.
1. The weather was supposed to be nice.
2. The park was having a special nature program.
3. He had a new fishing pole.

Pauline was late for school.
4. There was a power failure during the night.
5. Her brother cut his finger.
6. The car wouldn't start.
Linda's flower garden was beautiful.
7. She carefully planted the seeds.
8. She watered the garden.
9. She spent many hours weeding the garden.
Janice will become a math teacher.
10. Janice enjoyed teaching her younger brother.
11. She liked to help her teacher.
12. Janice's favorite subject is math.
Pp. 51–52
1. B
2. A
3. A
4. C
5. A
6. B
Pp. 53–54
1. C
2. D
3. A
4. B
5. B
6. D
P. 55 Answers will vary.
1. Nicole will ask her mother to buy her some glue.
2. Ted will go sledding.
P. 56 Answers will vary.
1. Roger will put his report into his bag.
2. Regina will get a kitten.
3. Cindy will write a letter to Katie.
Pp. 57-58 Answers will vary.
1. Doug and Justin will rake the leaves.
2. Tom will clean his room.
3. Adam and his parents will go to the new restaurant for dinner.
4. Diane and her mother will paint the room.
5. Sharon will call for help.
6. Carl will call David.
7. Elsie will ask her mother if she could wash the car to earn spending money.
8. Nancy will go home and go to bed.
P. 59 D
P. 60 Answers will vary.
1. Ron was enjoying his visit

to the zoo.
2. Diane was going to have a busy day.
3. Don enjoys the sailboat.
4. Juanita was a good speller.
Pp. 61-62 Answers will vary.
1. Teachers teach us many things.
2. Paula's dog can do many tricks.
3. Terri likes to read many kinds of books.
4. Wesley likes to take care of his baby sister.
5. C
6. B
7. D
Pp. 63-64
1. B
2. B
3. C
4. D
5. C
Pp. 65-66
1. C
2. C
3. B
4. A
5. B
P. 67
1. By the noise they make when they are scared.
2. They lick damp leaves.
3. Answers will vary.
P. 68
1. twisters and cyclones
2. central plains of the United States
3. almost always come in the spring
4. 250 mph
5. warm air from the south crashes into cooler air from the north
6. tear up trees and flatten towns
Pp. 69-70
1. drinking, cleaning, and keeping us cool
2. two thirds water
3. one quart of water
4. a half trillion gallons a day
5. 115 gallons of water
6. 4,000 gallons
7. hawks, falcons, and eagles
8. a sharp claw
9. Raptors need to be able to find small animals to eat.
10. move from one area to another
11. in the spring

12. in the north
Pp. 71-72
1. D
2. A
3. D
4. C
5. B
Pp. 73-74
1. B
2. A
3. C
4. D
5. B
P. 75
a. 4
b. 3
c. 5
d. 6
e. 1
f. 2
P. 76
1. a. 3
b. 6
c. 1
d. 2
e. 4
f. 7
g. 5
2. a. 3
b. 7
c. 1
d. 6
e. 2
f. 5
g. 4
P. 77
1. wormlike larva
2. The larva finds shelter in a log.
3. The larva keeps warm using its antifreeze and shelter of log.
4. The larva becomes active.
5. It becomes an adult beetle.
P. 78
1. preheat oven
2. mix flour, baking soda, salt, sugar, nutmeg, and cinnamon
3. stir in water and cooking oil
4. stir mixture until the ingredients are blended
5. bake for one hour
6. let bread cool before removing from pan
Pp. 79-80
1. C
2. C
3. B
4. A
5. B

Pp. 81-82
1. D
2. B
3. A
4. B
5. C
P. 83 Answers will vary.
1. Charles and his friends went fishing.
2. Charlotte stayed all night at Nicole's house. They watched a scary movie and had trouble sleeping.
P. 84 Answers will vary
Pp. 85-86
1. B
2. D
3. A
4. C
5. C
6. C
P. 87 Answers will vary.
1. The weather was getting colder outside.
2. Betty was getting ready for bed.
P. 88 Answers will vary.
1. Paul did not do well on the math test. Karen made a high score.
2. Steve's house had burned to the ground.
3. Bob and Vicki had had a quarrel.
4. Jennifer had celebrated her birthday with a party with her friends.
Pp. 89-90 Answers will vary.
1. Karen is in the hospital.
2. Tim is putting away all the camping equipment.
3. Diane saw her parents coming home.
4. Carla had been shopping.
5. Tom had broken his leg.
6. Eddie's mother had come home from the hospital with a new baby.
7. The day was the Fourth of July.
8. Fall was coming and it was getting cooler.
Pp. 91-92
1. B
2. C
3. C
4. A
5. C
Pp. 93-94
1. C
2. C
3. A
4. B
5. D

Answer Key